REVIVING SACRED SPEECH

Reviving Sacred Speech

The Meaning of Liturgical Language

Second Thoughts on *Christ in Sacred Speech*

Gail Ramshaw

Generously Donated By:

___Rev. John West___

OSL Publications
Akron Ohio

REVIVING SACRED SPEECH
The Meaning of Liturgical Language:
Second Thoughts on *Christ in Sacred Speech*

Copyright © 2000 The Order of Saint Luke
Third Printing - March 2004
All rights reserved

ISBN 1-878009-36-2

This book is printed on acid-free paper that meets the
American National Standards Institute Z39.48 Standard

Produced and manufactured in the United States of America by
OSL PUBLICATIONS
P. O. Box 22279
Akron, Ohio 44302-0079

Editor: Nancy B. Crouch, O.S.L.
Cover design by Laura R. Bidwell, LR Designs

Biblical quotations, unless otherwise noted, are from the Revised Standard Version of the Bible, copyright 1946, 1952,
© 1971, 1973 by the Division of Christian Education of the
National Council fo the Churches of Christ in the U.S.A. and
are used by permission.

The Order of Saint Luke is a religious order dedicated to sacramental and liturgical scholarship, education and practice. The
purpose of the publishing ministry is to put into the hands of
students and practitioners resources which have theological,
historical, ecumenical and practical integrity.

Contents

Introduction *15 years retrospect*

In 1985 I wrote *Christ in Sacred Speech*, a book about the metaphoric meaning of liturgical language. The book has been out of print since 1994, but since people still find it a helpful primer on metaphor in the words of Christian worship, OSL Publications inquired whether it could reprint the work. However, I know that in the last fifteen years I have read steadily and thought incessantly on these matters, and on many specific issues I have second thoughts. Consequently the publisher and I came to this decision: we would reprint the original book, but with an essay added onto each chapter, on how my thinking has evolved. I am grateful to Nancy Crouch, O.S.L., for the opportunity to re-issue the book as *Reviving Sacred Speech*, my first and my second thoughts on metaphor in liturgical language.

On some of my original positions I stand firm. I remain committed to the weekly eucharistic worship of the Christian Church and to a liturgy that is both shaped by centuries of Christian tradition and informed by today's speech. I continue to probe the method that metaphor employs to enrich our minds and alter our behaviors. Mediocre Sunday worship notwithstanding, I persist in the belief that there is more height and depth to ten minutes of the classic eucharistic liturgy than we can know or perhaps bear. As a Christian considering liturgical language, I approach that ancient yet still luminous burning bush, and there in that small tree glimpse among the mysterious branches the wood of the cross, aflame with the fire of the Spirit. I trust that in that fiery tree there is life for us all.

In two areas especially there has been significant development in my thought. Let me begin with my title. I am aware that usually the publication of a book's second edition retains the original title. However that title itself, *Christ in Sacred Speech*, is something about which I have second thoughts. The original title indicated my theological formation. From Martin Luther on, Lutherans have

ix

attended to Christology with fierce denominational
fervor, and this christological focus was apparent
throughout my early writing. However, in especially the
last five years I have sought to surround my Christology
with a vibrant and orthodox trinitarian theology. Now-a-
days I wish that even Lutheran sermons would conclude,
not with Christ, but with the Spirit and the manifestation of the Spirit in the Church. I have found, Sunday by
Sunday, that as I attend to the Trinity, the liturgical texts
of the liturgy are deepened, widened, renewed. I trust
that the book's new title reflects this revitalization of
liturgy that trinitarian theology has given me.

pneuma

Secondly, I have read the writings of nineteen hundred years of Christian women. I was startled to read in
the Prologue of *Christ in Sacred Speech* that I acknowledge by name only five men and several groups of
persons that at that time were overwhelmingly male.
Now, however, whenever I consider liturgical language, I
hear also the visionaries, led by Perpetua; the poets,
guided by Hildegard of Bingen; the mystics, such as
Julian of Norwich; the preachers, for example Jarena
Lee; the feminists, headed by Lucretia Mott; and contemporary female theologians, a shelf full of them. As well, I
am accompanied by feminist Christian liturgists who are
struggling with the undeniable and endlessly troubling
fact that much of our beloved classic liturgical language
is androcentric from its core out. My task is no longer
only to recognize the liveliness in historic texts, but also
to revive any life in and around them that androcentrism
has smothered.

In fifteen years my prose style has changed. I now
write less objectively than I did back then, with more
pauses, more qualifiers, more voices echoing through my
head that deserve to be recorded: lots more commas. I
can only hope that this two-tone prose will not prove
disconcerting to the reader. At least you will always
know which decade the remarks represent.

Before I lay out the plan of the book, I will do what I
did not find so necessary fifteen years ago: define "the
liturgy." When this book speaks of the language of "the
liturgy," it means the words of the traditional texts of the

Western rites of eucharist and daily prayer. These texts have developed over the centuries and are represented by the standard service orders of a growing number of contemporary Western Christian denominations. In the West, these texts are not a Sanskrit, frozen words from a sanctified past, but are continuously reworked so that the ancient metaphors can speak of God's mercy to us in a contemporary tone of voice. Some Christians, indeed, some entire denominations, dismiss the value of the Church's traditional patterns of worship and combinations of metaphor, reserving to themselves the responsibility of composing their own worship texts. This study will prove helpful mostly to those who use the classic liturgical texts, although perhaps Christians who do not will discover what they are missing.

Some readers might find a definition of "metaphor" helpful. Words are used in human communication in a variety of ways. Some language serves to label, with the goal of precision in communication; some language expresses emotion and thus communicates attitude and personality. Some language is socially powerful speech, in that saying the words effects a new situation: "I take you to be my husband" is an example of what linguists call "performative utterance." But human speech is always straining to say new things, to speak of realities that escape our current labels and reach beyond purely personal expression. For such communication, metaphor is the best linguistic tool humans have.

In metaphor, we convey A by saying B. The hearer, who knows that A is not B, is surprised to discover that B actually conveys A amazingly well. The hearer encounters A in a new way because of the linguistic surprise of B. An example of metaphor from religion is the statement, which is untrue, that God is a Rock: the hearer realizes that, yes, God is indeed a Rock. Metaphor is called "figurative language" — that is, I superimpose a picture (a "figure") on top of what I wish to communicate, and my picture conveys my meaning and my emotion. The more metaphors in a sentence, the more like poetry and less like prose that sentence is. "We pray for healing" is a prose sentence. "On either side of the river is the tree of life with its twelve kinds of fruit, and the leaves of the tree are for the healing of the nations" is a poetic sentence containing one metaphor after another. Although some scientific thinkers, such as Aristotle, disparage metaphor as being an unnecessary layer on top of truth, frosting covering up the cake (that's a metaphor), many contemporary theorists of language understand that this layering of meaning, this addition of interpretation by talking of A as if it were also B, this ability to make metaphor, is the primary distinguishing feature in human communication. The frosting is the best part. Religion, which is perpetually trying to speak beyond normal categories, is replete with metaphor.

Now, from the original Prologue:
    While a full interpretation of liturgy requires examination of music and movement, architecture and personnel, symbol and culture, this study focuses on liturgical language. The move to contemporary American English from Latin and Jacobean English showed us that the meaning of the liturgy's words is a more complex issue than lexical definition. The words of our worship find their meaning in the context of the whole liturgy. We must inquire into religious history, Judeo-Christian symbol, biblical languages, liturgical development, cultural patterns, and contemporary vocabulary. Liturgical language functions within this complex metaphorically, and in order to analyze liturgical language at its various levels, we must first understand how metaphor functions.
    The first chapter will examine the liturgy as human speech, a system of words. Liturgy is rhetoric, public speech declaimed for persuasion. Liturgy also is metaphoric. Metaphor occurs when speech superimposes two disparate images. Language about God must needs be metaphoric, for human language has no words that precisely describe divinity.
    Chapter 2 discusses the sacred in Christianity, suggesting that we find the sacred in a christological crossing of theophany and offering. Chapter 3, then,

holds together the concepts of the sacred and of speech. It is easy either to take refuge in the sacredness of liturgical language and conclude, "This is truth," or to apply sophisticated theories about metaphor in order to conclude, "This is not truth." Liturgical language, Christian sacred speech, goes beyond both critiques to say, "This is the way we name truth." When we ask whether a liturgical phrase has meaning, our answer has to be "yes-no-yes."

We then apply this liturgical hermeneutic to some two dozen liturgical texts. Chapter 4 investigates the divine names integral to Christian liturgy, discovering roots in ancient religion; tracing the revelation, the history of translation, and interpretation; and offering the specific Christian meaning for these names. Chapter 5 both explicates our primary metaphors for God as found in Psalm 95, the *Agnus Dei*, and *"Veni Creator Spiritus,"* and deals with the controversial question of feminine metaphors.

The next three chapters deal with Christian sacred speech as it describes the liturgical event. Chapter 6 focuses on sacred time: the week, the year, and the day. Chapter 7 discusses sacred speech about place, seeing especially in the *Sanctus* and *Benedictus* a complex metaphoric presentation of Christian holy space. Chapter 8 examines our sacred speech concerning holy things, especially bread and wine and baptismal water, and discusses a contemporary description of "what goes on" during the eucharistic prayer. Chapter 9 focuses on the liturgical language that describes the Christian assembly. "We are dead," says Ash Wednesday; "we are alive," says the baptismal invocation; "we are one with the needy," say our intercessory prayers; "we are one with the saints," says our sacral calendar.

Chapter 10 outlines catechetical implications. For the baptized child, the maturing adult, and the whole assembly, the liturgy is the Church's vehicle towards growth in grace. A liturgical homily is a school for the sacred speech proclaimed in the lessons. Finally, in the epilogue, tired of all these words, we consider liturgical silence as the logical end of our metaphoric speech.

And as for second thoughts:

Each chapter will conclude with an essay, sometimes short, other times extensive, in which I indicate in what ways my mind has changed or how my thoughts have developed. At the close of the book, after the printing of the endnotes, I have provided "A Second-Thoughts Bibliography," a list of the books that, in the last fifteen years, have most significantly contributed to my evolving positions on liturgical metaphor.

May my willingness to admit to you all that my earlier thoughts need correction and nuance, more knowledge and more wisdom, be a small example of the Church's need continually to revive its understanding and usage of the historic metaphors in our worship. I dedicate this book to my treasured colleagues in the North American Academy of Liturgy, whose continuous support of my work for over twenty years has been water to the tree that is me.

Gail Ramshaw
Begun on the Day of Basil, Gregory and Gregory, 1999
Concluded on Mary Magdalene's Day, 1999

Liturgical Language as Speech

RHETORIC

Speech is an essential ingredient in Christian liturgy. Not by any means the sole ingredient, speech is mated with symbol, and accompanied by music and ritual. For liturgy to be liturgy, this complex occurs within the assembly before God. Those Christians who thought that speech constituted the entire liturgical event suffered through painfully barren worship, for even a longer and longer sermon cannot replace symbol, music, and ritual. But for worship to be Christian, symbol, music, and ritual must be focused by specific speech: speech to God, about Christ, about the event, about the assembly.

Speech is composed of words, yet it is more than words. Words have individual entries in a dictionary, but even though words have many denotations and even more connotations, we sometimes fool ourselves by believing that the dictionary can tell us a word's definitive meaning. Speech is communication, words in combination, address exchanged. In speech each word bears on each other word. Within the context of speech we discover which of the many possible meanings of each word is appropriate. Thus it is more accurate to think of liturgy as speech than as words, for in the liturgy words find their meaning in the context of the sentence, the hymn, the prayer, the whole rite, and the assembly. The words themselves — words like "heaven," "grace," "offer" — are diamonds in their many facets. Theological dictionaries exhaust themselves giving the Hebrew, Greek, Syriac, and Latin roots, the biblical use, and the theological definition of the key words in the Christian vocabulary. As well, there are the secular meaning and the contemporary connotation. Yet in the liturgy these multivalent words are set beside other complex words, and the speech that results from the

incant/ecstasis

interrelationships between these words calls us into lively scrutiny and living faith.

The speech of our liturgy derives from the incantatory chants and ecstatic exclamations of earlier religions.[1] The very rhythmic power of the communal song transformed the consciousness of the participants and, it was hoped, called forth the attention and perhaps the mercy of divinity. In ancient religious chant it was not that certain words effected certain conditions, like in medieval magic. Rather, the people's participation in powerful speech was strong enough to alter their perception of the universe and perhaps the universe itself. Contemporary Christian hymns, chants, mantras, and choral responses, as well as the sung liturgy, are a rationalist concession to ancient orgiastic rhythms. Yet even our staid contemporary music and rhythm alter religious speech, and while here we study words on a page, the incantatory power of holy words when sung full voiced in the faithful assembly constitutes a dimension this examination of speech can hardly touch.

The speech of the liturgy is not primarily doctrinal speech. The liturgy is not constructed out of a systematic theology, although a systematic theology of sorts can be constructed from the liturgy. Indeed, like Cyril of Jerusalem in the fourth century, several theologians in our time have heeded the often-cited principle, "The rule of prayer establishes the rule of faith," and have built their theological systems out of the liturgy.[2] But doctrine and systematic theology are third-order language, abstract philosophical speculation that organizes thought into consistent and logical categories. Such third-order language is written for the rational mind to absorb; its syntax is not meant for communal recitation, and it need not be intelligible to the ear. Instead, liturgical speech is a combination of first- and second-order language. First-order language, the exclamations of human communication, we find in exchanges such as "The Lord be with you." Second-order language, the narratives recording human exchange, we find in the lessons. The creed is the closest thing in the liturgy to doctrinal speech. It was a late addition to the liturgy, and optional

2

besides. More important, within the liturgy this third-order language functions not as intellectual abstraction but as communal exclamation: "We believe!"

Nor is liturgical speech primarily poetic language. Poetry is subjective; it exists in its own right for itself. Poetry does not need any outside point of reference — the original audience, for instance — to be legitimate. In fact, even if there is an outside point of reference, the greater the poetry, the less significant the reference point. It does not matter to whom Shakespeare addressed his sonnets, and the biblical sources for Dante's *Divine Comedy* or Milton's *Paradise Lost* do not account for the greatness of the poems. A poem needs no "meaning" apart from its inexplicable esthetic effect. On the other hand, Christian liturgy is not written by a single self-reflective consciousness. Liturgy must have reference beyond its own beauty. So it is that committees working on liturgical revision have not been well served by contemporary poets and that poems inserted into the liturgy as prayers or responses are risky business. So too, hymns composed by demonstrably great Christian poets may require liturgical revision. No, liturgy is not poetry.

Nor is liturgical speech colloquial. We have learned this lesson during ten years of flimsy liturgical dialogue like "May the Lord get through to you." Not even in the secular world do we elect current conversational tone when the communal situation is socially significant. Colloquial speech is dictated by individual feeling; it changes rapidly in a fast-moving culture. The presider's cheery greeting "Good morning!" may be offensive to those suffering recent loss. In such a case the colloquial speech has fragmented rather than united the assembly. Liturgical speech ought to be vernacular, but vernacular is not the same as colloquial. The formal conventions of a marriage rite ought to be altered by the vernacular to reflect women's rights, but that is quite different from the couple's colloquially extemporizing immature reflections on love. No, the liturgy is not colloquial speech.

Although not colloquial, Christian liturgical speech at its best is vernacular. Christian speech is not a Sanskrit, a wholly other language required and reserved for

3

Vox Clara "Vouchsafe" "and with your spirit"

sacred purposes. To the extent that Christians rely on
transliterations and archaisms in liturgical speech, our
incarnational theology is in trouble. Christianity has
from its inception struggled to translate the parent
languages of Hebrew and Aramaic into the vernacular.
Paul wrote in Greek. Theology was systematized in
Latin. Reformation insights were articulated in German,
French, and English. Christian speech is vernacular with
a twist: the language of faith is a dialogue between our
contemporary experience in its vernacular dress and the
gospel as written in the Scriptures and repeated in the
tradition.[3] We must use common speech to proclaim good
news that is outside our common experience. The recasting of liturgical speech or the fine tuning of a eucharistic
prayer is a momentous task: one must know the gospel,
the tradition, and the contemporary situation, and must
hold them together in liturgical language.

If liturgical speech is not dogmatic prose, poetic
monologue, or colloquial conversation, then what is it?
The category of rhetoric will serve well. Sometimes, of
course, "rhetoric" has a pejorative connotation, the lies
of Hitler having given the skill a bad name, the folksiness
of television having displaced the classic art. Instead let
us recall rhetoric as the ancient Greek art of using formal
language eloquently in order to persuade. For the liturgy
does intend to persuade — to praise God, to remind God
of our need, to plead for mercy, to remind ourselves of
our faith, to call one another into faithful living. The
persuasive character of worship is clearly seen in Pente-
costal services, where the preacher exhorts God and the
people in expansive tones and the congregation cries out
its "amens." But all worship has its roots in persuasive
rhetoric. Jewish liturgy reiterates the praise of God and
calls down God's justice on the world. As the liturgy of
John Chrysostom says, "Again and again in peace let us
pray to the Lord." The adoption in the West of formulations of court address for the Christian prayer of the day
also indicates a sense of prayer as effectual speech of
persuasion.

Detailed rhetorical analyses tend to be technical and
dull, and this study of liturgical language need not con-

4

centrate on the craft of rhetorical writing. However, it will be useful to discuss rhetoric briefly, for the term has fallen on hard times. For Aristotle, rhetoric meant instructions for effective debate. For eighteenth-century linguists, rhetoric meant rules of elevated grammar. In contemporary America's predilection for casual and idiosyncratic speech, the word is seldom used. But some philosophers and critics are now attempting to resurrect the category of rhetoric.[4] The concept can be useful in tuning our ear to liturgical speech, for it signifies attention to words, images, syntax, and structure.

In the art of speaking effectively, one chooses words thoughtfully. It is not that one matches words to discrete meanings, for words have their denotation and connotation in combination with other words — all the more reason that word choice is a difficult task of discrimination. Words in rhetorical speech require a gravity of acceptability, yet they cannot be so ponderous as to sink underground. The vocabulary in religion deserves special consideration, for religions are, among other things, traditions of words, words translated from original languages, words with a long history of meaning and devotion. Thorough analysis of Christian liturgy requires fluency in Hebrew, Greek, and Latin; in the languages of the European and English Reformers; and with contemporary novelists and poets. What were and are the meanings and the feelings of these words? This is the first consideration for the critic of rhetorical speech.

In the art of speaking effectively, one judges imagery. Which images assist in eloquent speech, and which do not? What are the sources of the most effective imagery? Rhetorical speech will have little use for imagery grounded solely in personal experience, since for its communal purpose rhetoric must rely on common sources for imagery. C. G. Jung suggests that the images most powerful in human consciousness are not innovations but are ancient mythic and religious symbols shared by all humankind.[5] If Jung is correct, archetypes like light and water are significant even for those who have not read the Bible and Milton. Let us hope that Jung is right.

Rhetoric is also the art of shaping syntax carefully. The lines we so often hear quoted from Winston Churchill — "Never in the field of human conflict was so much owed by so many to so few," "I have nothing to offer but blood, toil, tears, and sweat" — are masterpieces of syntax. Syntax concerns itself with design, balance, and euphony; with the placement of words, the amount of tension in the lines, and the tone of the phrase. Superb syntax approaches beauty. We think of the stately yet lively balance in Thomas Cranmer's translations and original collects. Note the exquisite simplicity of this work of Cranmer's:

> O Lord, which for our sake didst fast forty days and forty nights; Give us grace to use such abstinence, that, our flesh being subdued to the spirit, we may ever obey thy godly motions in righteousness, and true holiness, to thy honor and glory, which livest and reignest . . . .

Or:

> Almighty and merciful God, of thy bountiful goodness, keep us from all things that may hurt us; that we, being ready both in body and soul, may with free hearts accomplish those things that thou wouldst have done; through Jesus Christ our Lord.[6]

Cranmer spoke sixteenth-century English, and while its taste in syntax is not the same as ours, we are wrong to conclude that eloquent syntax is inconsequential in contemporary rhetoric.

Finally, the art of speaking effectively involves the matter of structure. Generally, rhetoric is not extempore. It is ordered and crafted into a form that is balanced and appropriately weighted. Rhetoric takes time to speak and to hear, and over that period of time the structure of the prose becomes a set piece of effective eloquence.

All this talk of eloquence and balance may sound like the last gasp of a dying English teacher, but we must shout, "Hear! Hear!" and heed the deathbed plea. Since contemporary American English meets few situations similar to corporate liturgy, our task of agreeing upon the rhetoric for this generation of the Christian assembly is especially difficult. Some stylistic decisions made in the last twenty years — to drop the "to" in consecutive infinitive phrases, to drop the "You who" formula in the prayers of the day — were argued on the basis of the principles of colloquial speech. But liturgy is rhetoric, and as elevated and eloquent speech it has its own rules. We are still discovering what those rules are.

METAPHOR

meaning

This study of liturgical language seeks to inquire into meaning. What does the speech of the liturgy 'mean'? Philosophers in this century have suggested various ways to think about meaning in language. Some early forms of linguistic analysis had conceived of words as labels and had hoped for unambiguous definition, as if words like numbers could precisely describe reality. Northrop Frye has traced the history of Western speech and demonstrates that the exercise of construing language as specific label has run its course.[7] Words cannot be the unambiguous descriptions for which we may search. Some Christian scholars have employed the insights of J. L. Austin,[8] applying his categories to their analysis of prayer, praise, and liturgical language.[9] But neither has this approach to linguistic analysis helped much in the religious understanding of the speech in public worship.

Increasingly in the twentieth century, philosophers *poet* of language view human speech with a poet's eyes. It is as if these students of symbolic expression followed C. G. Jung, who began as a psychiatrist and ended a mystic. *myst* But not only mystics and poets subscribe to this school of metaphor: Paul Ricoeur's massive synthetic studies have given the consideration of metaphor all the intellectual weight it may previously have lacked.[10] Ricoeur and other philosophers seek to move our concept of metaphor beyond the notion of Aristotle and his followers (including Thomas Aquinas) that it is mere decoration.[11] Aquinas' analysis of religious analogy and metaphor is based on a contrast between imagistic language and a basic language of factual accuracy.[12] Thus metaphor was long thought to be pleasant though unnecessary substitution of an image for an idea, the claw foot on the chair leg. Ah, but even in the common noun "leg," we have metaphor. Metaphor makes new mental reality. By seeing something old or new in terms of something else, metaphor changes everyone's perception from that time forward.

More than a few junior-high-school teachers have done us no favor by defining a metaphor as nothing other than a simile without "like" or "as." Metaphor, far from being merely a decorative figure of speech, is the fundamental unit of creative thought. In metaphor the mind expands in a fresh way, imagining the new and renovating the old. Metaphor does not label: it connects in a revolutionary way. Metaphor is not merely an image, the look-alike, the reflection in the mirror. Rather, metaphor forms a comparison where none previously existed. Metaphor alters perception by superimposing disparate images. A metaphor has been called "an affair between a predicate with a past and an object that yields while protesting."[13] The two images are logically incompatible. What shall we call the four sticks holding up the chair seat? How about "legs"? We speak scarcely a single sentence without relying on the metaphoric quality of language. Hidden inside our prosaic talk about chair legs is an ancient personification of the simple chair, a metaphor of lively limbs on dead wood. Such an openness to a history of transposed and superimposed meaning is most apparent in poetry. Not surprisingly it is the poets and novelists who keep speech continuously birthing for the next generation. In George Orwell's *1984,* complete governmental control of language in Newspeak is possible only because creative writing has been eliminated from the culture.

The school of metaphor seeks to understand where the metaphors originate, how the connections were made, what kind of reality results, and what the relationship is between the universe of speech and the universe outside speech. This approach to human speech is increasingly significant in theology and liturgy.[14] The metaphoric approach in analyzing expressions like "God

8

the Father" and "heaven" will occupy us constructively
for a good while. What is the father image? Where does it
originate? How is it used by Canaanite religions, Judaism, Christianity, medieval Europe, contemporary
America? What is the psychological effect of this metaphor? What is the relationship between Father as a name
for God and the being of God? Multiply these questions
by the number of words in the liturgy, and multiply that
by the number of interrelationships born of the liturgical
context, and you have an inquiry into the meaning of
liturgical language.

LITURGY AS METAPHORIC RHETORIC

We have arrived at the category for liturgical speech:
metaphoric rhetoric. The liturgy is rhetoric, communal
speech of formal eloquence. The liturgy is metaphoric, its
words, phrases, and sentences functioning within a
creative tradition as the symbols of our faith. Thus, to
analyze the meaning of liturgical speech we must ask
questions of rhetorical purpose and of metaphoric meaning.

Textbooks of rhetoric urge writers never to mix
metaphors. That is, one does not begin the sentence
galloping on a charger and conclude the sentence by
running out of gas. One metaphor should be safely in
port before another is launched. But in liturgical speech
metaphors mix freely.[15] In the phrase "Jesus Christ is
Lord, to the glory of God, the Father," the metaphors line
up next to one another so fast that for most people they
march by undifferentiated from one another. Jesus is the
given name Joshua; Christ recalls the Hebrew plea for
the Messiah; the metaphor of lord is Christianity's most
complex, applying the Hebrew name for God to the risen
Jesus; glory can be explicated differently with help from
Exodus or from John; and the metaphor of father has
innumerable interpretations. The rhetoric of Christian
liturgy relies not on metaphoric purity, but on the mingling of metaphors. The exegesis of the liturgy is much
more complicated than the explication of a poem by
George Herbert, in which the cleverness of the meta-
physical conceit lies in the sustained adherence to a

single dominant metaphor. In Christian liturgy the metaphors are myriad.

In liturgical speech both metaphor and rhetoric must serve a hospitable unity of the assembly. The symbolic language strives to be, like the rainbow, symbolic in a primordial way. Of course, liturgical speech, like T. S. Eliot's *Waste Land,* also calls out for footnotes, and this study will provide some such annotation. But if the liturgical speech is not on the deepest level symbolically accessible, the glosses will do little good. The unity of the assembly is served in the first place by the human metaphors below glosses: water, bread, wine. In the same way the rhetorical character of liturgical speech must serve the hospitable unity of the assembly. Liturgical rhetoric ought suggest to us not so much Jonathan Edwards's sermons — monologues declaimed — as a public conversation between the President and the Queen: significant speech exchanged warmly.

We learn this metaphoric rhetoric from the Gospel of John. The primary anthropomorphic metaphor of God in the Hebrew Scriptures is of the One-who-speaks. John's Gospel adopts this image of the speaking God by beginning with the words, "In the beginning was the Word." Speech is a fundamental path between the Judeo-Christian God and God's people. Christian contemplative mysticism is not a rejection of words but a journey through words, up the path of speech, on towards God. But this word became flesh. God took on the metaphor of a first-century Judean male, so that when we speak of Jesus, we speak, as in all metaphor, simultaneously of two different things at once: the life of a Jewish man and the being of God. On Holy Cross Day, the festival on which, incongruously, we revere the despised cross, we recall John's Gospel: "And I, when I am lifted up from the earth, will draw the whole world to myself (John 12:32)." On first hearing we are delighted by John's rhetorical skill. But the metaphor is astonishing. Jesus draws us upward to God by drawing us towards himself, as he is lifted up to God by being lifted up onto the cross. Rhetorical eloquence, abounding metaphor, such is liturgical speech.

10

SECOND THOUGHTS

Concerning rhetoric: That liturgical language is best understood to be formal rhetoric is a perspective more urgently needed now than fifteen years ago. More and more Christian assemblies accept it as their right to alter in slight or significant ways the liturgical speech of their denomination's published Sunday service orders. Most of this emendation is inspired, probably unconsciously, by television's speech patterns, in which highly skilled professionals either read a carefully crafted text as if they were speaking off-the-cuff or have acquired fame because they have a talent for conversing colloquially in memorable ways. In consequence of our incessant exposure to this kind of pseudo-informality, much casual talk is replacing the rhetoric of classic liturgical speech. All too often, this talk is devoid of image, shallow in theology, sentimental in emotion, and not nearly as humorous as the presider thinks it is.

My travels have taught me that many people around the world distinguish the language called "English" from that which they call "American." In the past, I used to write about "American English," but now, emboldened by this worldwide perception, I am beginning to speak of the American language. American is distinct from English in especially three ways: its innovative spirit in vocabulary, its relative rejection of androcentric conventions, and its preference for informality. I am aware that I write and speak more informally than do British Christians. It is necessary, then, continuously to test whether we are so close to the edge that we are falling off. A church in Copenhagen at which the great Danish hymnwriter N. F. S. Grundtvig served for awhile was built, inspired by the Baroque theaters of the time, with tiers of box seats along the sides of the room for wealthy parishioners. We now see this aberration as an inappropriate inculturation of the liturgy. Too casual a speech in the Sunday assembly is another example of overwrought inculturation, a miscalculation that impoverishes the

11

assembly with words too minimal for God and too narrow for God's people.

Concerning metaphor: Much in our society urges speech toward literal precision. Perhaps it is computer technology, despite all the good that comes from it, that is in part responsible for our society's increasing incompetence in metaphor. If everything can be stated as either plus or minus, metaphor, which always partakes of both, gets left off the screen. The rise of fundamentalism within and outside Christianity is another example of this choice for literalism, as if at least in religion A means only A and not in some way also B through Z. One group of Christians asserts that Father means Father, God said so, and so as a Christian you are required to say it. Meanwhile, another group responds that the word Father cannot refer to a nurturing God, and so as an enlightened person you ought never to say it. Both groups are literalizing the metaphor, by giving the word a single unambiguous referent. Ambiguity, the method of metaphor, is a turbulent sea. A fish pond might be easier, but the vocabulary of Christian liturgy is the Atlantic and Pacific combined.

Let me offer you one of my favorite illustrations of liturgical metaphor:

In 1968 Seymour Leichman published a remarkable children's story entitled *The Boy Who Could Sing Pictures*. In a poor medieval land, a boy named Ben discovers that when he sings out happy metaphors, such as the river, the rainbow, the sun and the spring, miraculously the pictures appear, bringing the peasants joy. When Ben is forced to sing for the wicked king, he sings sad metaphors, "carpenters without wood, snowflakes in a blind beggar's eye." The king decides to have Ben executed, and with all the people gathered, Ben sings once more:

> He sang sugar cane from another country, melons and cherries and all summer fruit in the winter snow. . . . And on and on he sang the Promised Land. The weary, he sang rested. The hungry, he sang full. The cold, he sang warm. And the great sadness, he sang all away.

12

The song turns the king's heart to justice, and the story concludes with the entire population treated by the king to "a simply marvelous breakfast in the meadow."

This story has provided me with an image of the liturgy. Ben's songs for the poor are our opening praises of God; Ben's evocation of suffering, brought on by the presence of the evil king, is our intercessory prayer; and the grand song at the end, before the simply marvelous breakfast, is our eucharistic prayer. Along with the author Leichman, I believe that metaphors are miraculous: they not only superimpose a new interpretation onto an old reality, but they can actually effect changes toward the Promised Land. I believe that at the Sunday liturgy we receive the metaphors from the Bible and from the Christian past. These metaphors transform us and our perception of and vision for the world.

Concerning meaning: Just as with rhetoric and metaphor, "meaning" is a less secure category than it was fifteen years ago. Postmodernism suggests that since universals do not exist, meaning is more arbitrary than not. Studies of especially non-Christian ritual have familiarized us with traditions of religious language that do not have "meaning" in the Western, post-Enlightenment, self-reflective-consciousness way in which I speak of "meaning." In some of the world's religious traditions, ritual seeks to alter the person's consciousness by means of repetition of relatively arbitrary verbal formulas. I continue to maintain, however, that Christian liturgical language intends to create and celebrate genuine communal meaning. It recognizes the mercy of God come into this world, and it inspires lives of integrity and justice. If I am proved wrong, if I become convinced that there is no meaning in liturgical language beyond the self and its imagination, I will stop going to church on Sunday morning, and find something to do that does indeed have meaning.

Concerning the Trinity: Fifteen years ago I concluded my first chapter with Christology, by citing as an example of metaphoric rhetoric the Johannine reading appointed for Holy Cross Day. Now I think far more trinitarianly. For example, in explicating Holy Cross Day,

13

richer fare

I would argue now that the liturgy does not give us only one passage written by one man, John, about another man, Jesus. Thanks to the Spirit of God working in the Church, we have the lectionary offering us a full menu of images for the festival. In the Spirit there is a multiplicity of voices: joining with the metaphors of the Johannine community is the bizarre story from Numbers 21 in which an ancient goddess memory has been reinterpreted in order to proclaim the mercy of a different god; a Hebrew psalm borrowed for Christian liturgy, through which, in typically Christian paradox, we claim to see God's "right hand and holy arm" on the transverse beam of the cross; and Paul's discussion of the wisdom of the cross. The celebration of the day recalls Queen Helena's archeological dig in the fourth century and her discovery of what she believed was the True Cross. And what do we mean by John's talk of "the Son of the Father"? (I think of the exchange in Chaim Potok's novel *My Name is Asher Lev*: the Hasidic boy, mystified by all the depictions of the crucifixion in the Brooklyn Museum, asks his mother, "What does that mean, the son of the Ribbono Shel Olom?" "I don't begin to understand it," she responds.) To help us know what we and John mean by "the only Son," we'll sing together hymns about the cross, "The Royal Banners Forward Go" by the sixth-century Italian Venantius Fortunatus, "There in God's Garden" by the seventeenth-century Hungarian Kiraly Imre von Pecselyi, and "O Blessed Spring," by the twentieth-century American Susan Palo Cherwien. The Spirit crowds us all together around the cross, with transformative rhetoric, metaphor on top of metaphor, a tree of life after all. The Church comes to know "the Son and the Father" only in the Spirit, together with all who suffer, together brought to God.

More True.
Than Chy—.
Via Lect.

14

Liturgical Language as Sacred

THE SACRED

Religion is on the rise again. Post-Enlightenment
secular humanism stands stunned by our wars and our
Holocaust. We have seen that both the Enlightenment
expectations for a harmoniously evolving and rationally
based world order and the Romantic ideal that "everything that lives is holy" were naive and arrogant
assumptions about human capability. Our century has
witnessed a revitalization of popular religion and a new
public status for religious leaders. Intellectuals are
returning to faith. The phenomenologist Rudolf Otto
used the word "numinous" to talk anew about our
nonrational perception of transcendence.[1] Scholars like
Mircea Eliade, the historian of religions, C. G. Jung, the
psychologist, and Clifford Geertz, the anthropologist,
helped academia to respect the study of religion again.[2]
Fifteen years after writing *Secular City,* Harvey Cox
wrote *Religion in the Secular City.* Secularism has not
conceded, but religion is able more freely again to assert
itself in the marketplace.

Religion is predicated upon a world view of bivalent
reality, of the profane and the sacred, the common and
the holy. Religion sees levels of truth, levels of existence.
The common level is one accessible to all and rudimen-
tary to life. The deepest level is marked out as sacred, set
apart by its relationship with the divine. Sacred time,
sacred space, and sacred objects all participate in that
deeper reality because divinity has therein visited the
world or because humanity has therein offered itself to
God. The ancient stories do not make it clear which
came first: did the object become sacred because God
touched it, or did the object call down God's grace because it was first ritually dedicated? A sanctuary is
sacred for both reasons. The building, dedicated to the

honor of the deity, is transformed. It is also able to transform because of the presence of the deity. Religions hope that by contact with divine life the devout will participate more fully in reality and our profane existence will be to some degree redeemed and energized.

THE SACRED IN CHRISTIANITY

Neither the Israelites nor the Christians invented the sacred. They took over existing notions of the sacred from prior and neighboring cultures and significantly altered them. A sacred place, a sacred time, a sacred object became a vehicle for grace and an experience of the divine love and so was appropriated by the Judeo-Christian tradition in accordance with its own perception of God as benevolent. The story of the sacrifice of Isaac (Genesis 22) is one such narrative. Here a current practice, a sacred ritual to appease the deity by slaying the firstborn, becomes the occasion for the revelation of a gracious God. Yet the incident is not over. The metaphor of sacrifice remains paramount in the Hebrew tradition, leading to the central Jewish religious festival of Passover, and, for Christians, to the cross and the Eucharist. Traditional religious symbols of the sacred have been reinterpreted as vehicles for the grace of our God.

Many such stories can be cited. Jacob's dream of the ladder (Genesis 28) is an important memory for the Israelites, for here again God claims the people and promises them a blessed future. But all the ingredients of this Hebrew sacred event are familiar to scholars of ancient Near Eastern religions. Jacob's ladder sounds very like a ziggurat, a stepped pyramid like the many used to approach and appease God. Yet here the ladder becomes the vehicle for God's gratuitous blessing, which descends on the runaway Jacob. The use of stones to mark a sacred place is a common feature in ancient religions. Jacob's stone is seen anew by being anointed as holy to the God YHWH. Israel's building of the temple is another such example. Many of its architectural details remind scholars of the Egyptian temples to the sun god.

Solomon's dedicatory prayer (2 Chronicles 6) praises the LORD, the God of Israel, who is greater than this present house, who nevertheless deigns to dwell here in order to bless the people. When Elijah wins his contest against the prophets of Ba'al (1 Kings 18), he has called down God's power by using the same sacred pattern as the Canaanites: a bull to be sacrificed to God. The sacred mountain of God, common in ancient religions and usually the highest local hill, is for Judaism not even geographically located. Yet this is the Sinai (Exodus 19:20) on which Moses received the law in a storm of thunder and lightning, and the Horeb (1 Kings 19:8) on which Elijah heard God speak in a still small voice. The mythic mountain has become one of several real places to hear the word of God.

In each of these examples the two components of the sacred are held together. First there is theophany: here God has revealed God's self. The people have heard or seen God, on this mountain, at this sacred stone, in this temple, and so this place is called holy. But also at this place the people have offered something to God: a lamb, prayer, incense. The religious ritual itself renders the place holy. The abiding characteristic of the God of Israel and of Jesus is this: that even our meager offerings are accepted by a beneficent God because God has already come down from divine heights to save us. Religion has been met by grace, and we get the Christian sacred. We do not magically harness God; rather, our faithful praise discovers God's gifts already given.

This pattern continues in the New Testament. When the hemorrhaging woman is healed by touching Jesus' garment, Jesus tells her that her faith has made her well (Mark 5:34). Religious symbol has met with grace. The mythic image of a sacred tree, common in ancient mythologies and present in the Canaanite rituals of the asherah pole, echoes in the Garden of Eden's forbidden tree of life (Genesis 3:22) and in the tree of life with its twelve fruits in the heavenly city (Revelation 22:2). But in the New Testament the tree of life is the historic cross of Jesus, from which issues the life of the world. The bronze serpent that Moses sets on the pole (Numbers 21:9) — surely a borrowing from Canaanite fertility rituals — heals with the grace of God, as does Jesus on the pole of the cross (John 3:14). When Christians talk of the crucifixion as the central sacred event of history, we use language both of offering — Christ sacrificed himself for us — and of theophany: here preeminently we see the grace of God.

In light of this incarnate God, New Testament Christians alter once again ideas of the sacred, changing Israelite symbols to make them more reflective of the mystery of Christ. Paul suggests in Galatians that the sacred is no longer a definitive category, but since people require some sacred avenue, Christians may in freedom select it nearly arbitrarily. Yet a pattern of the Christian sacred emerged quickly enough. The sacred day is not the Sabbath, sanctified by God at creation, but the first day, the eighth day, renewed by Christ in the resurrection. The sacred festival is not the Passover of a Hebrew historical memory, but *Pascha*, the celebration of Christ's resurrection. Old distinctions about kosher were gradually abandoned, but a new sacred food took over, the food of the last supper, the body and blood of Christ. The elaborate vestments of the priesthood gave way to simple white robes, a sign of baptismal identity with Christ. "Holy things for the holy," calls out the Orthodox priest, and the people reply, "One is holy. One is the Lord Jesus Christ, to the glory of God the Father." What is sacred in religion and what was holy for the Jews has met up with the cross.

If the sacred in religion is the place or moment or object of contact with — and thus transformation by — God, in Christianity that contact is always marked by Christ. Incarnation assures us that contact with God does indeed embed itself in human time, human space, created things. But the key is always the cross, the turning power always grace. The Church must always be inquiring whether its layers of sacral reality point to and emanate from Christ. So the grove of trees creating a numinous space is less likely a Christian sacred space than is the single bare cross in the sanctuary or three unadorned evergreens in the nave at Christmastide. Ecstatic music as well must ask whether the hearer is led toward or away from the mystery of Christ. Liturgical art is not merely religious art but art that points the assembly in faith to Christ.

Yet this is not to say that Christianity has no need for the sacred. The claim that "Christianity is not a religion" is a helpful corrective when the Church forgets the incarnation and sells its soul unreflectively to what is culturally construed as sacred. But claiming that Christianity has no sacred is as inappropriate as adopting "the sacred" uncritically. The incarnation does not do away with the sacred; rather, symbolic objects are more likely than not to be conveyors of divine life. It is not that, as a religion, Christianity sanctifies a small bit of life as offering; it is rather that, because of the incarnation, religion takes over life and hallows the creation. The inquiry as to whether the sacred is first appointed by God or first consecrated by ritual, the choice between theophany and offering, is answered in the cross. A man offers himself, and this is theophany. When Jesus blesses God with bread and wine, we call it offering; yet we call it theophany when God is made known in the breaking of bread. As Jesus offers himself and God is revealed, the Church has its sacred food; for at the intersection of offering and theophany the Church finds its liturgy. Jesus is both the offering and the theophany, the one who gives himself to God and the one in whom God is revealed.

CHRISTIAN RHETORIC

To construct Christian rhetoric, then, we have two tasks. On the one hand, sacred speech records theophany. Since we have no unalterable, unadulterated sacred speech but are continually translating and recasting our liturgy, how can new expressions tell the old story with fidelity? On the other hand, sacred speech constitutes offering. Can we agree on contemporary language suitable for praise? Banal language cannot record theophany; otherworldly language cannot serve in praise and offering.

praise Then petition
prophecy Then offertory

The liturgical rhetoric we have inherited from the
Jews is marked by an interchange of praise and petition.[3]
Many psalms contain such a pattern: first praise then
petition (Psalm 27); first petition then praise (Psalm 22);
or a weaving together of the two (Psalm 63). Because we
trust in God's grace, because we see ourselves in the light
of a history of gracious action, we are bold to plead and
we offer our petitions. Solomon's prayer (2 Chronicles 6)
praises almighty God, and then prays for all sinful and
suffering humanity. Ezra's prayer at the reinstitution of
the feast of Tabernacles (Nehemiah 9) both praises God
for Israel's salvation and pleads for mercy anew. At his
Passion, Jesus prayed to God both in willing surrender to
God's grace, "Abba" (Mark 14:36), and in the agonizing
lament of his desolation, "Eloi, Eloi" (Mark 15:34). With
similar paradox we proclaim pericopes from the Sermon
on the Mount, hard sayings about our offering of the
ethical life, and we conclude by acclaiming, "This is the
gospel of the Lord!" Theophany and offering coincide.

The syntax of our worship is diverse. The lessons
alone offer the Hebrew poetry of the psalms, the Greek
verse of John's Gospel, the expansive narrative of the
Joseph cycle, the subordinate clauses in Paul's expository
prose, the incongruous imagery of the Book of Revelation. Add to these the court-petitionary tone of Christian
liturgical prayer, the imaginative meditations of
mystagogic homilies, and the cadences of fine speech in
Greek, Latin, German, French, and English, honed by
the centuries. Hymns of different ages speak their own
rhetoric. In Lent alone we have the mythic imagery of
Fortunatus's "Sing My Tongue," the personal piety of
Bernard of Clairveaux in "O Sacred Head," the eucharistic piety of Aquinas in "Of the Glorious Body Telling,"
the Reformation theology of Paul Gerhardt's "A Lamb
Goes Uncomplaining Forth," and the American black
communal lament in "Were You There." Christian rhetorical styles abound.

But to be Christian liturgy, the sacred rhetoric is to
be communal rhetoric. Even though the gospel is heard
by the individual, God comes to bless the whole people.

20

Much Christian poetry is not appropriate rhetoric for liturgy because it speaks of experience so private that it cannot become metaphor for corporate praise and prayer. Although psalms can function as private meditation, as Christian liturgy they speak of Christ and the Church. Christian rhetoric always proclaims God's grace to all the people. The prayer ascribed to Teresa of Avila, "I am not surprised you have so few friends, considering the way you treat them," is clever and memorable but hardly communal rhetoric.

In a time of many Bible translations and accelerating biblical research, it is not self-evident which is the sacred vocabulary for our rhetoric. We are very far from a universal recognition that certain words are the sacred words, too sacred even to pronounce. Rather, we contemporary Christians do not agree whether the tetragrammaton is appropriate to our liturgical prayer, whether Lord is a culturally conditioned title, or how *Abba* should be translated. We struggle to decide which words are essential for Christian rhetoric and which, culturally determined and far removed by time and place, are best abandoned for the sake of the incarnation. Furthermore, even when we agree on the essential Christian vocabulary, contemporary words change from under us constantly. No sooner have we an energetic translation of a psalm than the meaning of the word "gay" changes. A decade after a graceful translation is published, our pronoun system is in chaos. Thus, finding the sacred vocabulary is not easy for contemporary Christians.

CHRISTIAN METAPHOR

Christian metaphor takes the principles of metaphor one step further. That is, metaphor applies the inappropriate name and so surprises us with truth. Christianity takes words already inappropriate in a religious context and lifts them to the cross.[4] We know, for example, that in many ancient Near Eastern cultures the king is granted the title Son of God. By extension, religions of the Near East apply the human title of king to the deity.

This anthropomorphism is admittedly metaphoric. Yet in Christianity we do one better, for John teaches us to apply the divine metaphor to Christ. Christ is king when he ascends the throne of the cross. Thus our God can be called Sovereign, not because God wears a crown in the sky, but because Christ reigns from Calvary.

Most Christian metaphor follows this pattern. Language with which the Hebrew people spoke of God and themselves is reinterpreted in light of the resurrection and the Church.[5] As Christians redefined an existing sacred vocabulary and reassigned meaning to an existing sacred imagery, a new religion was born. "God is a rock," the psalms say, evoking a secular word in a startling metaphor. "Christ is our rock," Christians say, applying Hebrew sacred speech both to the crucified and risen Jesus and to God. Because of Christ the sacred metaphor takes on new levels of meaning. That Israel is a vineyard is metaphor enough. Yet we say that Christ is the vine and that his blood is our wine. Thus we superimpose the death on the cross over the majesty of the divine and speak distinctly Christian metaphor.

Our task is both to recall the strangeness of our metaphors and to bring them to the cross. Realistic pictures of Jesus dressed as if he were king blur the Christian message. Christ is better enthroned on the cross or acclaimed on a donkey. When we get lazy in our metaphors and turn their strangeness into easy images, we need again the religious vision, the "ontological flash,"[6] that breaks all religious metaphor, a second time, over the cross of Christ. Thus when we speak about the Christian assembly, we call ourselves a family, brothers and sisters in Christ. But that is only a metaphor, and if we facilely believe in that metaphor as if it were an objective description, we might find ourselves forgetting the loneliness of individual Christians, the rupture in any Christian assembly, the divisions within the Church, and human alienation from God. For even Jesus on the cross cried out in his abandonment by a distant God.

All our essential metaphors are found in the Scriptures, and there we focus our study. The theological interpretations of Christology and the explication of the

Trinity that find resonance in the liturgy had their rhetoric formed in postbiblical times, but very little of our liturgical language requires explication from the history of doctrine. While the centuries have added upper floors of meaning and interpretation, the solid foundation lies in the Bible. It is as if the liturgy were the edifice of San Clemente in Rome. The present-day church, home for American tourists and devout Italians, was built in the twelfth century; it is adorned with art of later times, medieval mosaics and Renaissance frescos. But this church was built on top of a church commissioned by the emperor Constantine. Yet Constantine's fourth-century sacred space was built on top of a wholly ordinary apartment house, a place that was revered as sacred because there, tradition says, Peter's disciple Clement met with other Christians to read the Scriptures and to feed on Christ. Excavations discovered that Clement lived down the block from a Mithraic temple. Like San Clemente, our liturgy goes down deep, arises alongside the rites of other religions, assembles the faithful around word and sacrament, and acquires layers of interpretation as the centuries pass. Some layers illumine and some dull the mystery of Christ. Let us go exploring the language we call sacred to find the mystery of Christ.

SECOND THOUGHTS

My chapter suggested that the Christian liturgy is the intersection of theophany and offering. I now judge this definition as a helpful way to describe Christology, but it is rather too flat, too axial, God up there and Jesus down here, for Trinitarian faith. This two-way street needs to acquire a third dimension. Perhaps it would be better to think of the Christian faith and its liturgical expressions as the intermingling of theophany, offering and communion.

In Christianity, theophany discloses a single plurality. God has revealed divinity to be triune. Christians encounter the one God not as a monad, one entity all by itself, but as a trinity. The single divine life is complex,

23

embracing within itself also the humanity of Jesus and the assembly of the Spirit of Christ. When Christians wish to experience a manifestation of God ("theophany"), we look to Christ and to one another who, gathered in the Spirit of God that was sent forth in the resurrection, embody the Spirit of God in the world. There appears before us not a single point of divinity, but three interlocking circles.

In Christianity, offerings, those gifts humans think they are giving to God, are in a surprise move transformed. Jesus offered himself to others, and finally to the reality of death, but we discover on Easter evening that his body is alive and shared by the assembly. There is not only the cross, a single point of offering, but the worshipping assembly, meeting on the day of the resurrection, made alive by the Spirit of that offering, presenting food not to God, but to the poor.

In Christianity, then, this meeting of theophany and offering creates — could we picture it this way? — a cylindroid vitality. Like the spiral of DNA, the interweaving of the two creates a column of life, a space for communion. Yet this communion is not just any old mutual admiration society, in the creation of which we humans are endlessly engaged. It is our communion with all who suffer, our relatedness towards justice. Our circle includes always more persons and causes than we seem capable of embracing.

Here is a picture of cylindroid Christian liturgy: In Lohja, in southern Finland, is a church fully illustrated with fifteenth century frescos. On the vaults of the ceiling are depictions of significant Old Testament narratives; around the walls is the life of Christ; on each side of each pillar is a saint; and interconnecting them all with the worshippers in the nave are the swirling branches coming from the Jesse Tree that surmounts the entrance door. The building speaks of theophany, for the paintings retell all the stories of God's mercy to the people; it represents offering, for the magnificent structure was erected and decorated in praise to God; and it effects communion, for the worshippers with the saints are caught up together onto branches of the tree that illustrates Christ's place among the people. Such a biblical tree fantasy is far better than a pole.

My chapter contained considerable talk about "the cross." These days I am less facile with lines like "The key is always the cross," "Jesus offered himself to God," or "Christ sacrificed himself for us." Like "Gesundheit," these are words we are trained to use, and while I continue to use them, I see it as one of my tasks to figure out what they mean. (Snoopy barks, "Woof!" Linus asks, "Woof? What's that supposed to mean?" Snoopy thinks, "I don't know. It's just something everyone is our family always said.") Jesus was executed. We might say that he offered himself for the healing of others, for the feeding of the poor, for the revitalization of stagnant religion. Together, inspired by the Spirit, we must reflect what we mean by traditional phrases like "he offered himself to God" or "he gave himself to take away our sin." Clearly, this language has lost its meaning for countless numbers of persons in our society. Perhaps we need to interpret such language more persuasively. For those people trained to bow the knee at the name of Jesus, one can say simply, "the cross." But fewer and fewer people have been so trained. The cross needs to get some body to it. That body, it seems to me, is the Church made alive in the Spirit. The transformation of the universe by the cross is enfleshed by the body of the Church — unfortunately, as both church history and parish reality demonstrate, not very well.

Some such widening cylinder, replacing the pole, will help us correct the tendency in religious life to identify the sacred with the male and the profane with the female. Lots of religion, ancient and modern, superimposes its pole of sacrality onto its socio-economic ladder. What is more like the divine is, naturally, higher on the pole. For everything that is less like the divine — women, bugs, dirt — the task of becoming connected with the sacred is more difficult, if not impossible. Religion has often been used as the holy vehicle for bumping ourselves and others higher or lower up or down the sacred pole. Characteristically, in this age-old religious exercise, women did not make out very well. The current interest in wicca only reverses the polarities, so that the female, by being closer than the male to the sources of life, is closer to what is divine.

Thus Christians must beware of the category "the sacred," not only because we recognize in the unjust execution of a poor man a re-definition of the term, but because in baptism the old boring understandings of who is holier than whom, the too-typical notion that I am better than you, these are turned upside down. And it is not only ancient religion from which we must distinguish ourselves. Much New Age religious practice is classic gnosticism reclothed in romanticized robes or tattered jeans. Oftentimes in our culture the desire to become sacred, to get to a place other than this world, represents, not so much the Buddhist meditation on life as suffering, but rather the mundane realization that other people are a pain in the neck. Talk of "the sacred" can be only sanctimonious speech for a focus on the self. But quite the contrary is the case in Christian liturgy. When the presider calls out, "The peace of the risen Christ be with you," the "you" is a plural pronoun. Perhaps we have to start saying "you all," to make more clear this Christian countercultural idea: the sacred comes not to me, but only to us.

The Paradox of "Sacred Speech"

MYSTICS

If rhetoric and metaphor are the categories most appropriate for our consideration of liturgy, and if the sacred in Christianity is a christological intersection of theophany and offering, how then can we put "sacred" and "speech" together? How is it possible for human speech to convey the divine? Either of two opposing positions is easy to maintain. The secularist affirms the human origins and historical development of religious speech and thus dismisses its sacral character. On the other hand, the popularity of fundamentalism shows that many people choose to believe unreservedly in the words of their religion. They find security in divinizing religious language, and they cannot tolerate ambivalence in its interpretation. How can we maintain the balance required for sacred speech?

The biblical witness acknowledges that God is beyond human speech. God's revelation to Moses (Exodus 3) is described as a fire which does not burn. Like many other experiences of the divine, this one escapes human categories. The voice of God is heard, giving a name that centuries of linguists and theologians cannot translate. The name is an open, nonrestricting name. Who is God but a fire which does not burn, a voice from the bush, a word unpronounceable, a name that does not define. This Hebrew narrative acknowledges that human language cannot adequately describe God. Yet the text affirms that God is our God and that God has a name which, although it escapes our grasp, is nonetheless spoken in our ear.

The psalms, in imaginatively approaching the naming of God with metaphoric accolades, imply the unnameability of God. In Psalm 18, God is called

27

"strength," "rock," "fortress," "deliverer," "refuge,"
"shield," "horn," and "stronghold," and God is described
as a storm, a volcano, a mythic giant, a lamp, a judge,
and a general. The plethora of metaphors of God indicates a freedom in religious poetry and a healthy antidote
to our staid philosophical categories about the essence of
God. The New Testament Johannine writings carry on
the psalm tradition. In the Book of Revelation, language
proves quite inadequate to convey the vision. Words pile
on top of each other and fall over the edge of the pages in
a minglement of metaphor that is nearly absurd. A
woman with a crown of twelve stars? A marriage feast
hosted by a lamb with seven eyes? The sea tamed into
shimmering glass? The visionary's ecstatic utterance
invents extraordinary combinations of words because
theological formulae are inadequate for his experience of
God.

The tradition of Christian mystics continues the
ecstasy. In the sixth century Pseudo-Dionysius wrote
mystical words that exemplify the apophatic tradition,
the God-is-not sayings. God is not good, says Pseudo-
Dionysius, thereby making a statement not about God
but about the inadequacy of our category of the good. In
his *Mystical Theology* he calls the Godhead, It:

> Ascending higher we say:
> It is
> not soul, not intellect,
> not imagination, opinion, reason and
>   not understanding,
> not logos, not intellection,
> not spoken, not thought, . . .
> not being,
> not eternity, not time, . . .
> not spirit (as we know spirit), . . .
> It is not dark nor light,
> not error, and not truth.[1]

Pseudo-Dionysius urges us to let God be God rather than
to strain to make God the object of language's meager
categories. In the fourteenth century, Meister Eckhart
developed this *via negativa*:

Now pay attention: God is nameless, because no one can say anything or understand anything about him . . . . If I say "God is a being," it is not true; he is a being transcending being and a transcending nothingness. About this St. Augustine says, "The best that one can say about God is for one to keep silent out of the wisdom of one's inner riches." So be silent, and do not chatter about God; for when you do chatter about him, you are telling lies and sinning.[2]

The mystic tradition continues in Catherine of Siena. After one of her divine visions she wrote:

Can

SNTTER

O eternal Father! O fiery abyss of charity! O eternal beauty, O eternal wisdom, O eternal goodness, O eternal mercy! O hope and refuge of sinners! O immeasurable generosity! O eternal, infinite Good! O mad lover! . . . And what shall I say? I will stutter, "A-a," because there is nothing else I know how to say.[3]

Devout poets join the mystics in conceding the inadequacy of language. Dante wrote copiously about the torments of hell and the suffering of sinners: but when he experienced the light of God, he wrote:

But as my sight by seeing learned to see,
The transformation which in me took place
Transformed the single changeless form in me.

That light supreme, within its fathomless
Clear substance, showed to me three spheres, which bare
Three hues distinct, and occupied one space;

The first mirrored the next, as though it were
Rainbow from rainbow, and the third seemed flame
Breathed equally from each of the first pair.

How weak my words, and how unfit to frame
My concept — which lags after what was shown
So far, 'twould flatter to call it lame![4]

Even theologians talked about the unspeakability of God.
Augustine comments that if we think we understand
what we are talking about, it is not God we are talking
about! He writes:

> Have I spoken of God, or uttered His praise, in
> any worthy way? Nay, I feel that I have done noth-
> ing more than desire to speak; and if I have said
> anything, it is not what I desired to say. How do I
> know this, except from the fact that God is un-
> speakable? But what I have said, if it had been
> unspeakable, could not have been spoken. And so
> God is not even to be called "unspeakable," be-
> cause to say even this is to speak of Him. Thus
> there arises a curious contradiction of words, be-
> cause if the unspeakable is what cannot be spoken
> of, it is not unspeakable if it can be called unspeak-
> able. And this opposition of words is rather to be
> avoided by silence than to be explained away by
> speech. And yet God, although nothing worthy of
> His greatness can be said of Him, has conde-
> scended to accept the worship of men's mouths,
> and has desired us through the medium of our own
> words to rejoice in His praise.[5]

Thomas Aquinas himself, apparently after a vision of
God during the Eucharist one morning, refused to dictate
any more of his *Summa*, saying, "All that I have written
seems to me like so much straw compared to what I have
seen and what has been revealed to me."[6]

Fascination with the unknowability of God continues.[7] Yet we need words with which to pray. The mystics
remained tied to the language of the Church through the
liturgical life. While they wrote private ecstasy, they
attended the liturgy with their community. Their visions
often focused on the mystery of Christ. Julian of Norwich, much quoted these days because of her chapters on

30

divine motherhood, applied the image of mother to Jesus, whose death cradles us in love and whose blood is our nourishment.[8] When the mystical writings avoided the mystery of Christ and attempted direct access to God apart from the cross, the writings found themselves peripheral to the Christian faith. For in Christian mysticism the ecstatic utterance focuses on the preeminent paradox that we see God in Jesus.

THEOLOGIANS

But Christianity is not mainly a mystical religion. We cannot become so frustrated by the inadequacy of human speech that we deny its validity altogether. Already in Genesis 1:3 God is said to speak. Throughout the Scriptures the faithful listen to God's words, and this word of God is the basis of the faith. The poem that opens John's Gospel uses the metaphor of God's speech as the primary metaphor for Christ: "In the beginning was the Word"; "the Word became flesh" (John 1:1, 14). The word of God, the preached word of the prophets and apostles, the written word of the scribes and evangelists, and the prayed words of the worshiping community: in this tradition of word, Christianity develops.

Let us imagine the rabbis confronted with Exodus 3, God's appearance to Moses in the burning bush. Here is a story that escapes human categories. Yet the story must be proclaimed to the community: there must be a way to say the mysterious divine name. So where the text records the sacred tetragrammaton, the rabbis pronounced YHWH as if it were *Adonai,* a contemporary title of reverence and authority. The theologians have thus tamed the vision. What was unspeakable and untranslatable is given a vernacular word. The vision must be harnessed so that it can pull the whole assembly along together.

Not only must there be words about this God (theologos), there must be orthodox words. Orthodoxy is written by that tradition of theologians who affirm the past and restate it: "Yes, that is what I believe: this is how I say it." Heresy occurs when a person says of Christian doctrine, "No, that I do not believe: instead, I

31

would say this." Liturgy must express the consensus
about orthodox faith, so that to pray these prayers is to
be Christian. Although liturgical language is not identical
with doctrinal language, the faith expressed in the liturgy
is the faith we are called to believe. Thus while remembering the ecstatic utterance of the mystics, the liturgy
relies on the theological tradition to provide communal
understanding of the metaphors of faith. Liturgy strikes
a balance between the ecstasy of John and the logic of
Paul. Thus it is not surprising that when theologians
identify the God of whom they speculate, they quote
from the Church's liturgy for their language.[9]

YES-NO-YES

Liturgy is informed by both the mystics and the
theologians. In the liturgy we sing metaphoric songs, rely
on music, art, and symbol to express the inexpressible,
and admit the inadequacy of our language. But also in
the liturgy we confirm our specific faith in the cross of
Jesus and stand under that cross as Jesus stands under
his Father. The question is: How can we maintain these
contradictory truths? Is our language mystical or orthodox? How is this admittedly meager language affirmed as
truth? What is the meaning of sacred speech?

The hermeneutical method for the study of liturgy is
YES-NO-YES. Because our words are sacred, we say YES to
liturgical language. Because we revere the language as
holy, we take off our shoes and kneel down. We affirm its
truth and its meaning for our lives, devoutly responding
with a YES. But step two is required by our linguistic
sophistication. Our liturgical language is mere human
language. It is only speech, words in English or Hebrew
or Greek. These words cannot contain divinity or convey
the essential being of God. Our words are pitifully meager: step two is a disillusioned NO. But our sacred speech
is the language of faith, our tradition of grace. We are the
community that continues to receive God's life through
these words. These words are salvation for us. Step three
is our faithful response to the admittedly hidden God, a
hearty YES to the sacred speech given us.

Let us first consider step one, the reception of the speech as sacred. Baptized into the death of Christ, we receive this language as our basic vocabulary. Helpless as either a kicking infant or a dying adult, we exist before the mystery of God. Like the *tohuwabohu* of Genesis 1:2, that formless void of created matter, we confront God, the I AM of all time and space. And we kneel. We acknowledge the difference between who we are and who God is and we receive the sign of the cross on our forehead. *"Abba,"* we pray. "Thanks be to God," we say after the lessons. "Amen," we say upon receiving the body of Christ.

But then we apply to liturgical language the hermeneutical skills of the biblical scholar. We establish as best we can the original text. We attempt to construct the original situation, the better to understand the original theological meaning. We study the tradition of translation and trace the history of meaning. We see our sacred speech evolving in new languages, meeting religious needs of altered cultural settings. We inquire into its meaning in contemporary America, aware that words constantly change in significance and that symbols acquire new connotations. We apply this historical-critical method to, say, the image of God as rock. What was the original Hebrew image? How was it used in the narratives and in the psalms? How did the rabbis expound on it? How does the Jewish symbolic meaning relate to other ancient mythological rocks? What happens to that Jewish symbol in the incarnation? What about Jesus as rock, Peter as rock, the Church as rock, Golgotha as rock, Jerusalem as rock, Rome as rock, doctrine as rock? Only after all this study can we expound the many meanings in the morning psalm (Psalm 95), "Let us shout for joy to the rock of our salvation." Pages could be written on the metaphor of the rock. Yet compared with sacred speech like "Jesus is Lord" or "Christ is arisen," the metaphor of the rock is child's play. We have much work to do in tracing the meaning of our sacred speech.

This critical task often leads us to say NO. The Majorca storytellers begin their tales with the phrase

Aixo era y no era, "It was and it was not."[10] Even if the realization makes us insecure, even if we would like to be fundamentalists, we must admit that the language is not the full truth for which we had hoped. Critical biblical scholarship will not allow us to "believe in" the text. We know too much: God did not dictate the Scriptures or our latest liturgical text. As well, contemporary philosophers of language call us into honesty about the legitimacy of our truth claims. Our only response is meager indeed: to talk enthusiastically about metaphor! Yet even we must admit that metaphor is a naming that is not. God a rock? The modern cynic cites the fact that urban dwellers have not enough meaningful experience of rocks — except those behind glass at a museum — for the image to work appropriately. Even as an archetypal image of solid ground and stable protection in the wilderness, rock is extremely limited as image for the being of God. Far from bearing easy resemblance to God, rock may seem particularly antithetical to divinity. A rock is not alive, it has no consciousness, it is not free, it crumbles with time. And where was this rock during the Holocaust? No, God is not a rock.

Yet finally to be the community that meets weekly to praise God with Christian sacred speech, we take the third step. Yes, this is the language we use to name truth. This is the tradition of religious language turned on its head by the death of Jesus. We are the people who received God's grace through Hebrew, Aramaic, Greek, Latin, German, English. We pronounce God's name as Lord, and we claim that Jesus is Lord. Step two was, with Anselm, faith seeking understanding: "I desire in some measure to understand thy truth, which my heart believes and loves. For I do not seek to understand in order to believe, but I believe in order to understand."[11] But step three recalls Tertullian: "It is to be believed because it is absurd."[12] Belief is, after all, not knowledge. It is consciousness beneath and beyond knowledge. It is acceptance of a tradition of grace in spite of the 'No' forced upon us by the limitations of language. To claim that worshipers "believe in the Bible" means that they take to themselves the biblical metaphors for God, for the human self, and for human community, and so form themselves into an assembly around Christ. The psalms were recited in the concentration camps. Aquinas, abandoning his *Summa*, struck by silence, still celebrated the liturgy. The contemporary philosopher, having grappled with Friedrich Nietzsche, sings a *Te Deum* in fervent hope that through this sacred speech the real God is worshiped. Like the women at the tomb, there was first their devout adoration of God, second their disillusionment at the cross. But the third step propels them into a final YES, a belief in God and a faith in the resurrection that recasts their old categories, leaps over their doubt, and assembles them into the body of believers around bread and wine.

The final YES is both hard and easy. It is difficult to affirm liturgical language as sacred speech after the painful honesty of step two. It is hard to push always toward the balance so that no single interpretation distorts the truth of the metaphor. It is complicated, being true to contemporary experience while claiming to be formed by ancient symbols and traditional vocabulary. Yet such faith is also easy. It is the final resignation into God, the last abandonment of the critical task. It is at the end allowing the waters of baptism to wash us into God's life. It is conceding the paltriness of both our scholarship and our doubt. Such faith is easy in that it is a gift from God, the gift we call grace.

The gospel narrative of the temptation of Jesus has given us this method. The tempter knows well the Hebrew poems: the beloved metaphors promise that God's Messiah will feed the poor in the desert, will gather into his justice all the world's authority, and appearing suddenly in the temple, will perfect a priesthood for the Lord. The tempter asks Jesus to say yes to these metaphors of salvation. But no, Jesus cannot take them on, then, literally answering the tempter's teasing and our prayers' pleading. Then finally, yes: as Jesus goes on through his ministry and onto the cross he becomes food for the poor, life in our desert, justice for the nations,

35

king of the universe, bearer of the New Covenant, puri-
fier of the holy ones. YES, NO, YES: Christ in sacred
speech.

SECOND THOUGHTS

It is important to recognize that both mystical rev-
erie and orthodox theology need each other. Either one,
if proceeding out of sight of the other, loses its way.
Mysticism can become so lost in divine ecstasy that the
poor are forgotten; theology can become a branch discipline of philosophy, too busy thinking to praise. The
interrelationship of mysticism and theology is apparent
throughout church history. In the most influential writers in the Christian tradition, the Augustines who went
before us, both mysticism and theology speak their truth.
The theological systems of the Reformers were only
another way to say the mystical poems of the medieval
nuns, both groups affirming the power of divine grace
within the person, outside and even despite
ecclesiological understandings. In the contemporary
Church, it is perhaps hymnwriters who play the role of
mystics, offering to worshippers hundreds of metaphors
to deepen and widen our language of faith. Some of these
poems will be sung for two years, some for two centuries. The faithful will decide which metaphors support,
enrich and advance orthodox theology.

My chapter used the word "orthodox" more than
many people do. The word is proving problematic in a
culture that questions tradition, resists authority and
glorifies individual creativity. My city's newspaper
reported on a Lutheran woman who goes to church
rather regularly and also worships the goddess who is   *Syncr*
herself. Such examples of syncretism abound in our
society. Yet I maintain that the word "Christian" has to
mean something other than "nice," something specific
that can be compared and contrasted with other simi-
larly-definable religions. What is of course fascinating
about the word "orthodox" is that it means, not correct
doctrine, but correct worship. The word returns us to the

36

questions behind this book: What words do we use,
should we use, in Christian liturgy, and what do they
mean? When I use the word "orthodox," I imagine, not
Doctrine Police or a Supreme Theological Court, but the
family photograph albums and my grandmother's cut-
glass bowl. "Orthodox": this is the way we are because
this is the way we have been.

I continue to think that YES-NO-YES is the operative
formula for Sunday morning. Even liturgical theologians,
perhaps especially liturgical theologians, must resist the
NO on Sunday morning. To be Christian is to assemble on
the day of the resurrection and to practice once again our
insertion into the metaphors of grace. Even if we did not
design the morning service, select the propers and choose
the hymns, perhaps especially if we did not — that is,
even when the words are not exactly the ones we think
best and most profound — we still say YES on Sunday
morning and join together for theophany, offering and
communion.

About the NO: In a time of the resurgence of fundamentalism, it is not popular to speak a no to the imagery
of faith. Even in the churches' debates over the naming
of God, one sees Christians on both sides of the question
attacking one another with Bible passages, citing this,
quoting that, as if biblical warrant is an unassailable
indication that one's position is right. To search our
sacred speech for the best possible vehicles of grace while
also admitting the NO — accepting that all this speech is
inadequate to its task — seems antithetical. It is not easy
to affirm contradiction. But it is the obligatory stance of
those of us who attend to the metaphoric language of the
faith.

What I did not discuss fifteen years ago is another
kind of NO, the NO that voices genuine rejection of some
historic liturgical language. I recall that during my childhood my devout Lutheran father refused to sing the
concluding lines of the old translation of "A Mighty
Fortress." "Then take they our life, goods, fame, child,
and wife, let these all be gone, they yet have nothing
won": my dad said he would not sing as if "child and

wife" had won nothing. The new translation clarifies the referent of the second "they." Perhaps my father could sing the current translation. The Church does keep trying to improve its liturgical language.

There are many levels at which such a NO is sounded. Somebody decides which words the assembly will or will not say. At the parish level, two persons select five hymns or chants, and in so doing reject five hundred others. The preacher chooses the words to sanctify in preaching. Someone else, crafting the intercessions, can choose whether to call God "Mother." At the denominational level, some committee decides how often the words "Father" and "Lord" will be included in the rite. On the ecumenical level, a task-force of a dozen people revised the enormously influential three-year lectionary. On the worldwide level, Christian churches debate whether baptism rituals that utilize any other than the classic wording are to be considered valid. The church needs vehicles such as these for deciding NO once in awhile.

But recently there are more and more individuals who say their silent or vociferous NO: not that metaphor again, no more, and I shut my mouth. The pacifist will not chant the warrior psalms: the American abstains during parts of the King hymns; the feminist will say "Lord" only ten times per service. At least in our society, no matter what the parish council, the denominational publishers and the Faith and Order Commission suggest, Christian presiders and worshippers are saying NO to this or that sacred speech all the time, avoiding one term, substituting another. It is as if Christians feel personally authorized to decide which words are sacred. And although on Sunday morning I try to say YES-NO-YES, on Monday morning I am one of those who craft prayers for churchwide use, and so I must decide which words and phrases need to be set aside in linguistic museums as no longer helpful for nurturing resurrection faith.

One example: the word "hell." I was raised in a Christianity that had no doubts about hell. Indeed, its reality was what Christ's salvation was all about. Yet

more and more Christians no longer believe it exists.
Even as metaphor, hell is being discarded. And while
jettisoning hell can occasion passionate theological
debate, saying NO to hell does not much affect the Sunday
liturgy. The word is almost never used in the Church's
liturgical speech. Even the current translations of the
creeds speak with more historical accuracy of "the dead"
as what "hades" meant. The only liturgical use of "hell"
that I can think of, apart from hymn texts that may be
chosen, occurs in the various churches' translations of
Hippolytus' eucharistic prayer: that Christ "crushed hell
underfoot" — an image more effective if you know the
Eastern icon of the Harrowing of Hell, Christ standing in
triumph on the broken doors of hades, which are some-
how also the cross, and pulling up Adam and Eve into
paradise. (By the way, the depiction of this icon at Saint
Savior in Chora, Constantinople, proclaims an Equal-
Opportunity Resurrection, with Eve and Adam each
grasping one of Christ's hands, and Christ looking, not to
a preferred Adam, but out to us all.)

But Christians are busy saying NO to other words as
well, words that are far more central to our sacred
speech. I am a cautious participant in this project. While
I firmly believe that some words can no longer hold
trinitarian mercy very well — they are leaking all over
the place — I also firmly believe that most words can
work better than one might at first think. Furthermore,
what leaks for me might hold fast for you, and liturgical
language is not mine, or any presider's, to alter at will.
The liturgy belongs to all the faithful, who have a right
to know what words they will use in worship. I can only
beg of us all, myself included, two things: that even as we
say NO here and there, we do so as faithfully participating
members of the Sunday assembly; and that every decision to excise metaphor from liturgical speech be made
only after the widest-ranging consultation with the most
inclusive company of Christians possible. Perhaps the
changes we advocate will constitute improvements.

Thus any NO we say must be hesitant at first, a
Perhaps-NO for a century or so. We lessen without eliminating. "Mom," my daughter said, "you've got liberal

leanings with a conservative core." I have found this personality disposition useful for someone who proposes sacred speech for liturgical prayer. Furthermore, since I am a lay person who never presides at the liturgy, I cannot myself speak the words I write. To those of you who do, I urge ceaseless study, remarkable creativity, continuous restraint, and the wisdom of Sophia herself.

— 4 —
Names for God

The Christian religion identifies and worships a
specific divinity. Although there is a private dimension
to religious experience, Christianity is essentially corporate. The God we worship must therefore be named and
shared by the community. The sacred speech that has
passed down through the tradition identifies and names
our God. Our God is this one over here, not Ba'al, not
Zeus, not Isis, not economic determinism, but YHWH
God, called *Abba* by Jesus of Nazareth. Our first task in
explicating Christian liturgy is analyzing the names for
God. What is our God named, how, and why? What
about other names for God, like Mother?

Seldom do words have single self-evident definitions.
Depending on the context, words can mean many, even
contradictory things. However, we call those words
proper nouns which more precisely than most point to a
single referent. Although the word "writer" has several
denotations and many connotations, the proper noun
Abraham Lincoln refers almost unambiguously to the
author of the Gettysburg Address. A proper noun functions more like a label than does the rest of the language.
Christianity gives God proper names, nouns that while
not univocally, at least more than usually, refer clearly to
the God known by Christians. The primary names Christians use for God are "God," "Lord," "Father," "Jesus,"
"Christ," "Son," "Holy Spirit," and "Trinity." For Christians, God with a capital G can mean the whole being of
God or one person of the three. Some of these names
have other referents: the more referents, as with the
word "father," the more confusion in interpreting the
specific Christian meaning of the metaphor.

A fundamental religious question is, Who is God? A specific religion answers, *X* is God: *AB* said so. We look to the primary revelations in our tradition for the names of God. These are the metaphors so basic to the faith that they are codified into creeds, elucidated in theology, and evoked in the Church's public liturgy. Who do we say knew our God best, and what did they call God?

The Jewish tradition reveres Abraham as the father of faith, and it is to this patriarch that God is revealed as *El Shaddai* (Genesis 17:1). God changes Abram's name to Abraham and extends the covenant of blessing and promise. Abram hears new words, dons a new name, and receives a proper name for God. The narrative records the private religious experience of the man who becomes the people's patriarch. Written in Hebrew but etymologically perhaps an ancient Mesopotamian name, *El Shaddai* probably means "God of the mountain peaks." Abraham's experience is captured by a metaphor: he met the God who is as unfathomable as that distant peak of glory, as mighty as a mount in its power and beauty, as intimate as the emotional strength of the natural image. *El Shaddai* has traditionally been translated "almighty God." The image of the mountain has been lost, relegated to a footnote, but the translation has become a proper name for our divinity, almighty God.

Twice more this pattern occurs in the Scriptures. In the narrative of Moses' meeting with God (Exodus 3), Moses as a central figure of faith has a private religious experience — a vision of fire that does not burn — and the experience is expressed in language. "I am YHWH," the Hebrew records. The tetragrammaton might mean "I am who I am," or "I will be who I will be." Scholars cannot agree. Yet whatever the name for the mysterious burning divinity, the sound is too holy for tongues to handle. The Hebrew phrase becomes an acronym of four capital letters that is never pronounced. It is replaced by the common noun "lord," the title in ancient Hebrew for the male authority figure.

Liturgical speech in Judaism and Christianity has never used the tetragrammaton. Lately one stumbles over it now and then, conjectured vowels producing a pro-

42

nounceable word. The Jerusalem Bible popularized this innovation. Its asexuality is appealing; but its use will not help Jewish-Christian relations, for devout Jews judge it absolutely offensive to pronounce the name of God. Some Christians argue that in Christianity God is closer than in Judaism. Christ has removed the fence around Torah, and we are able to speak God's first name. That Christians can speak intimately with God is true; but there are other ways to achieve intimacy without spelling out the tetragrammaton as a divine name for sacred speech. Sacred speech always takes its present meaning in relation to its past: this liturgical principle alone would urge us not to switch to YHWH, or to the conjectured Yahweh, but instead to refine our use of LORD. The mysterious holiness of God's name, the incomprehensibility of God's being, is a truth balanced but not eliminated by the testimony of Jesus.

The third such naming of God occurs in the New Testament when Jesus, speaking Aramaic, calls God *Abba*. The pattern is familiar: the central figure of our faith has a unique experience of God, which is recorded in a vernacular metaphor. *Abba* is the child's loving parent, not "our father" but "my papa"; and now as then "my papa" is a startling title for divine address.[1] Mark 14:36 records Jesus' praying to God as *Abba*. Paul, writing in Greek to Greeks, quotes the old Aramaic: "When we cry, 'Abba! Father!'" (Romans 8:15). Matthew and Luke also rendered the surprisingly familiar Aramaic term as the Greek noun "father." Jesus' experience of the intimacy of God — one of Jesus' countercultural trademarks and perhaps one of the reasons for his downfall — expressed in the metaphor *Abba* was translated into the more religiously acceptable word "father" and so became part of Christian sacred speech.

From the narratives concerning Abraham, Moses, and Jesus, come the names "almighty God," "LORD," and "Father." The names are not as religiously awesome or personally revelatory as the narratives would indicate. Much has been obscured by layers of verbalization and translation. As we set out to reawaken awe before the face of God, we look to the narratives about Abraham,

Moses, and Jesus, because our tradition hails these three above all others as followers of God and interpreters of the faith. What was the experience that made Abram leave for a land he could not possess? What was the fire that did not burn? How could Jesus call the Holy One of Israel "Papa"? The metaphors of mountain, of inexplicable fire, and of the faithful parent overlap in the mingling of images describing the God who saves.

These three dominant names for God occur in the invocation of the historic Roman canon — *Domine, sancte Pater, omnipotens aeterne Deus,* "Lord, holy Father, almighty and eternal God,"— and in most contemporary prayers of thanksgiving. In some the names occur in succession: the *Lutheran Book of Worship* reads, "Holy God, mighty Lord, gracious Father." In others, like the Ecumenical Prayer, the names "Lord" and "God" occur in the preface and the name "Father" begins the body of the prayer. Thus at the beginning of the Great Thanksgiving, we pray along with Abraham, who obeyed the call (Genesis 12:4), with Moses, who received the Torah (Exodus 19:20), and with Jesus, who was the Word (John 1:1). As we eat bread and wine, we recall Abraham, who shared his food with three mysterious visitors (Genesis 18:8), Moses, who ate and drank with God on Sinai and did not die (Exodus 24:11), and Jesus, who breaking bread on Sunday evening, showed forth his wounds (Luke 24:31). The entire tradition of word and sacrament opens now to us as we call on almighty God, LORD, and Father.

However, the metaphors do not stay untouched by time. Both secular and religious use of these words change with the centuries and even with the decades. Indeed, all these names for God are under present scrutiny. Is our God in fact God? What do we mean by "God"? Is this God almighty? Granting the theological concepts of God's omnipotence and God's mercy, why does evil rage in the world? Many people find Job's agonizing doubt more convincing than his final acquiescence. Others, finding the idea of God tenable, cannot bring themselves to trust such a God as they see.

44

The word "God" is criticized today for implying
masculinity, and neologisms like "God/ess" have been
suggested.[2] While we must reject that part of the tradition that construed the noun "God" as masculine, we are
not well served by resorting to polytheistic categories to
name divinity. "God" is masculine and "goddess" feminine in those religions in which divinity is shared by
many beings, some exemplifying masculine and others
feminine sexuality. When we use a word like "God/ess,"
we have adopted polytheistic terminology that still
carries explicit sexual overtones. Furthermore, "God/ess"
is not a pronounceable word: we must, like the rabbis,
find a word we can pronounce. We are better served by
retaining the word "God" and, as with occupational titles
in our time — poet, doctor — purging from it inappropriate masculine connotation. Sexuality has to do with
procreation that is due to mortality. Sexuality involves
the desire to merge toward unity. This sexual understanding of being is not congruent with our knowledge
of God. The Judeo-Christian God is beyond sexuality —
immortal, with no need to procreate, and already whole
in love. Our present task is to locate the word God beyond sexuality rather than deeper within it.

More troublesome is the word "Lord." What shall
we do with this title? Already the title *Adonai* was a
metaphoric substitution for the sacred name. How can
we exchange the masculine image of authority for that of
burning being? Democracy has further denigrated this
title by linking it to an anachronistic and unenlightened
economic and social system. A contemporary proposal is
to render the honorific title as "the Sovereign One."[3] An
intriguing suggestion, "the Sovereign One" has an enno-
bling sound and suggests the awe of the God beyond
names. Many agree that it enhances the narrative of the
burning bush. But it proves ungainly in sentence structures, in liturgical language, and in liturgical music. As
many contemporary married women experience when
they juggle hyphenated last names, one must be convinced of the benefits before committing oneself to the
undertaking. It is unlikely that liturgical speech could
render Lord as the Sovereign One, and surely we must

keep the language of the lectionary as close as possible to
that of the liturgy. A further consideration is how much
we value a single Christian language, for surely many
Christians would refuse to translate this root metaphor
in a new way. Yet the problems inherent in "LORD" pale
next to those in the name "Father."

We can distinguish between different connotations
of the name "Father." The first, as metaphor for the
covenant, is almost the only meaning encountered in the
name's use in the Hebrew Scriptures. God adopts the
Israelites and loves them as children. In nearly every
instance in the Old Testament, "Father" is the title for
God available only to the especially chosen and loved
ones. Like other monarchies in the ancient Near East,
the Davidic dynasty is called into unique relationship
with God (Psalm 89:19-37): the king is chosen as a son
of God; by implication, God is father. When Israel repents and turns to God, the title of "Father" is evoked
(Isaiah 63:16), because in a patriarchal culture sonship
functions as a metaphor for covenant. The Book of
Wisdom states that God, a severe king to the sinner, is a
father to the righteous.

In the New Testament, the covenant relationship is
articulated in a new way by Jesus, and to express the
intimate relationship between human and divine, Jesus
called God *Abba*. When Paul uses the name Father as the
acceptable translation of *Abba*, he usually links it grammatically with the name Lord Jesus Christ (Ephesians
1:2, 3). That is, the covenant relationship begun in Israel
and manifested in Jesus is made available to the believer
through baptism. Because of our baptism we are bold to
say *Abba*: "Father" is not a natural name for God, or we
would not need to be bold. The name "Father" is logically inappropriate for divinity: God is neither human
nor male, and a term implying a personal relationship
with a human being and the creator of the universe is an
image for faith, not for logic. But the paradox of the
metaphor commends it to our faithful use. God is Father?
No, whether we want God a father or not, God is no
father. But yes, "Father" is one of the ways we name
God. It is not the sole name of God, it does not contain

God's being, and it can easily be misinterpreted to convey the wrong image. But our claim that we stand with Jesus at the cross is invitation to use father language.

But several other connotations stick to the name "Father." John's philosophical use of father-son language describes not our covenant relationship but Christ's identity. In John's Gospel, "Father" designates the divine origin of the *Logos* and metaphorically identifies Christ with God (John 1:14; 10:30). Beginning in the second century, the Christians countered Gnosticism's belief that the creator god was not the same god as the savior god by identifying "Creator" with "Father." Thus God as creator is father of the universe.[4] This usage, popular especially at community Thanksgiving Day services, is not biblical. It is stereotypical religious mythology, as is the image of God as mother birthing the universe. In the fourth century the formulators of the ecumenical creeds stressed the philosophical meaning of Father — Son — Holy Spirit in order to articulate the relationship of Jesus with God and the mystery of the Trinity. That is, the Father is the father of Jesus, and the Spirit is the spirit of Jesus.[5] Thus "Father" became the theologians' creedal name for God. Later, medieval theology, speaking in a patriarchal and authoritarian culture, used father language to describe God's dominion and our obedience. Although this connotation occurs very rarely in the Bible, Martin Luther explicated father language in this disciplinary way in the Large Catechism.[6] Sigmund Freud has articulated the psychological connotation of the father as the figure representing our rankling dependence and our murderous aggression. God the Father then becomes our neuroses projected into the skies.[7] Feminists protest the conscious and unconscious sexual bias of father language.[8] Finally, there is the experiential connotation: what was my father like, and how does the experience of that inadequate human male influence my image of God?[9]

We cannot ignore the resonances of father imagery in mythology, philosophy, patriarchal culture, psychology, and personal experience. We must learn to distinguish one connotation from another, stressing the specifically

biblical theological meanings and weeding out the inappropriate growths that choke the Christian message.
Some people are suggesting that we return to the use of the name *Abba*. Its accuracy is appealing, its memory of religious ecstatic babble attractive; but its remoteness from contemporary English is problematic. Yet we are required to make a faithful presentation of the *Abba* metaphor.

Because words change in meaning, sacred speech requires careful catechesis lest the tradition become unrecognizable before our ears. Always the stories of faith must be retranslated into the latest vernacular, always the metaphors explicated anew. Only well versed in the tradition are we able to choose among the connotations that present themselves before us. "Father" must mean both the *Abba* who inexplicably feeds and clothes the adopted sinner and the *Eloi, Eloi* who inexplicably abandons the holy one on the cross. Such is the Father whom our praises attend and at whom we rage. Other images — the mythological creator, the Greek philosophical progenitor, the authoritarian male, Freud's neurotic projection, or our own fathers — are largely inappropriate as metaphors for the one to whom we pray.

THE SECOND PERSON: THE *GLORIA IN EXCELSIS*

Popular Christian piety always has addressed Jesus in prayer. From the lepers (Mark 1:40) and Mary at Cana (John 2:3) to contemporary exclamatory praise, Jesus is invoked for aid.[10] But theologians repeat the ancient dictum that prayer is addressed, as Jesus instructed, to God his father. Christians believe that prayer is heard because of Christ and offered in the Spirit of Christ: thus the formula "to the Father through the Son in the Spirit."[11] But occasionally a prayer is addressed to Christ, and the *Agnus Dei* is a popular chant that gained acceptability. Yet the name of the Second Person fills the liturgy, for the road that skirts Christ is one that eventually meets a different God — an avenue not open to the orthodox Christian.

All the names and primary titles for the Second
Person have their roots in Hebraic metaphor, but in each
case, as befits the mystery of the incarnation, the metaphor has grown differently than the Jewish connotations
would suggest. For example, the name given to Mary's
son at birth is "Jesus." "Jesus" is the Greek form of the
Hebrew name "Joshua." Etymologically the name means
"YHWH helps"; popularly in the first century it meant
"God saves." Joshua was chosen by God to lead the
people in Canaan (Joshua 1:1-2). The image of Joshua in
the Jordan River (Joshua 4) recalls the people's arrival
into the promised land. Although the name means "God
saves," Matthew's narrative (1:21) says that Jesus will
save. Here is the Christian surprise: first, there is the
Hebrew metaphor, Joshua signifying the faithful leader
and the new land; second, there is a translation into
Greek and a change of focus that affirms the
christological mystery — that this Joshua of Nazareth is
the God who saves.

The roots of the title "Christ" are deep and complex.
The Hebrew word *messiah*, "the anointed one," appears
in the Old Testament first in verbal form. Aaron and the
priests are anointed to pray (Exodus 28:41); Saul and
the kings are anointed to rule (1 Samuel 10:1); the
prophet will be anointed to preach (Isaiah 61:1). Prophet,
priest, and king use the word "anoint"; yet it is as the
anticipated revolutionary king that the title the Anointed
One becomes culturally significant in first-century
Palestinian Judaism. "You are the Christ," says Peter
(Mark 8:29), meaning that Jesus is the expected monarch
of Israel. However, Mark's theology makes it clear that
Jesus on the cross looked nothing like the anticipated
Messiah. In Acts are apparent attempts at explanation. Is
it that in the eschaton Jesus will become Christ, or that
Jesus becomes Christ at the resurrection? No, the emerging Church redefines the name Christ and alters the
metaphor to point to the mystery of the man Jesus. Christ
then refers so completely and explicitly to Jesus of Nazareth that for Paul it functions as Jesus' surname. To
explain the meaning of Jesus we use the metaphors of
oil, the priest, the king, and the prophet. John's narrative

establishes this title at the very beginning (John 1:41); the synoptic Gospels show that the title of Christ was the focus of Jewish condemnation (Mark 14:61); and by this title we are named.

In the book of John, the climactic name for Jesus (John 20:28) is "my Lord and my God." In Thomas' confession, the term *kyrios*, which Mark uses as a simple title of respect, Master (Mark 7:28), is reinterpreted to signify the title of God. LORD, the name for God, that honorific substitution for the sacred tetragrammaton, is now applied to the risen Christ: Jesus is Lord. While the typeface may distinguish LORD as YHWH from Lord as Master, every hearing of the word now signifies a compounded mystery. God who is YHWH is called LORD; Jesus who is Master is called Lord. It is not Lord as a male master that is important in the Christian naming of Jesus. Rather, the transfer of God's name to the man Jesus signifies the christological faith.

Further, Jesus is called Son of God. In the imagery of royal lineage the name "son" signifies the ruler and the name "father" signifies God. The king was called "son of the gods" even in those cases where the god popularly worshiped was female. The names "Father" and "Son," of course, suggest the priority of the First Person. Thus the Nicene and the Athanasian creeds sought to clarify the seemingly contradictory language. The "son" image suggests both Mark's carpenter who is intimate with God and John's *Logos* who is one with God. Through baptism, the metaphor comes to describe believers who, as one with Christ, are sons and daughters of God. We all become Davidic kings in virtue of the death of the one Son of God.

The names for the Second Person — Jesus, Christ, Lord and Son — occur in the classic *Gloria in Excelsis*. This hymn from the 300s has been part of the eucharistic rite since the sixth century. In its current translation, "Glory to God in the highest," the hymn has eighteen lines, six of praise to the First Person and twelve of praise and plea to the Second. The hymn provides an excellent example of how names for the Second Person are related to the names for the First.

50

The hymn begins with the angels' song of praise on Christmas (Luke 2:14), in which the God of the Judean shepherds is lauded for sending "a Savior, who is Christ the Lord." The opening couplet connects praise to God with human well-being, recalling the creation story in Genesis 1. The following quatrain praises the "LORD," "almighty God," and "Father," rehearsing the names we expect for the God we worship. We praise this God "for your great glory." "Glory" itself is a multivalent term. We remember Isaiah's vision of God glorified in a golden temple attended by mighty angels (Isaiah 6:1-4). Sometimes Hebrew used "glory" as a circumlocution for the being of God (Exodus 40:35). But John uses "glory" to refer to the incarnation and especially to the death of Christ (John 17:1). The word "glory" moves the hymn from the First to the Second person. Line 7 then reuses the title "Lord," this time to signify the identity of Jesus Christ with YHWH God.

The following twelve lines address the Second Person as "Jesus," "Lord," "Christ," and "Son." Thus lined up in quick succession are the images of Joshua leading the people across the Jordan; the itinerant preacher named the God of the burning bush; the long-expected anointed priest, prophet, and king; and the king by divine right, the son of the heavenly king. Yet there is one more appellation. In line 8 we explicitly call Jesus God, and we recall the Johannine image of the Lamb of God (John 1:29) who takes away the sin of the world. In this moment of praise we anticipate "Lamb of God," for it is as the paschal lamb slain for this Passover, this eschatological victor who died on the cross, that we adore Jesus as Lord. We plead for mercy, since only because of God's mercy is our praise received.

But Jesus is not only the one slain but also the one vindicated; he is now "seated at the right hand of the Father." This metaphor of the resurrection and ascension is perhaps our most anthropomorphic. We sing as if God sitting on a throne has a secondary throne on the right side, as if Jesus were chancellor, God's right-hand man. The metaphor shares with other anthropomorphisms the danger of naive interpretation, but none of our images of the resurrection and ascension — Jesus suddenly appearing behind closed doors (John 20:19), Jesus rising up above the clouds (Acts 1:9), Jesus appearing to Paul near Damascus (Acts 9:5) — is at all adequate to the assertion of faith that Jesus is one with God. The image of God's right hand of power is at least as old as Psalm 110 in which the LORD establishes the Lord at the right hand of heaven's throne, promising him the ultimate victory. Our hymn uses the courtly term "receive our prayer," as if we, like Queen Esther, are creeping up to the throne, begging the monarch to hear our petition.

In the last sestet still addressing the Second Person, our praise returns full voiced. Christ is the Holy One, as we cry out with the madman (Mark 1:24), "I know who you are, the Holy One of God!" Elisha was called "a holy man of God" by the wealthy woman (2 Kings 4:9), but in Isaiah (60:9, 14) God is called "the Holy One of Israel." Again the name of God's chosen one and the name of God come together in this man Jesus. Jesus is also "God Most High." This ancient pagan designation for God comes from the story of Abram and Melchizedek (Genesis 14:19). King Nebuchadnezzar also gives praise to the Most High God of Shadrach, Meshach, and Abednego (Daniel 3:26). Along with Melchizedek we offer ourselves with bread and wine to God Most High. With the pagan king we praise the one "like a son of the gods," whose appearance in the fiery furnace recalls the God Most High in the burning bush. The final three lines are a trinitarian doxology cast with traditional prepositions. Jesus with his Holy Spirit is gathered into the glory of God, as the Son with the Father.

It is and has always been the scandal of Christianity that the first-century Jesus of Nazareth receives the name of God. Against this the charge of blasphemy was leveled (Luke 22:70-71); this is the foolishness Paul defends (1 Corinthians 1:23-24); to explain this John talks about the preexistent *Logos* (John 1); and it is this mystery the ecumenical creeds strive to articulate. Often in history critics have attacked this naming of Jesus as God. The first-century Jews assumed it contradicted monotheism; in the fourth and fifth centuries Arius and

Nestorius doubted that such language could be used of Jesus without destroying our idea of God.[12] Thomas Jefferson's deist rendition of the New Testament shows us an Enlightenment reluctance to divinize Jesus.[13] Post-Christian feminists cannot bring themselves to give a man the name of God.[14] All these objections are logically valid: religion and common sense long to cast out that Jesus who says "I am" (John 8:58). We cry out that this language is too extreme! But in each century those who deny these names to Jesus have moved to the periphery of or altogether outside the Church. For us it is to name Jesus as Lord, Christ, and Son, and to see in these names the cross as the sign of God.

THE THIRD PERSON: THE *EPICLESIS*

Traditional Christian liturgy addresses the Holy Spirit in prayer only in the hymns on Pentecost Day. We pray for, not to, the Holy Spirit. In Western liturgies the Spirit has little explicit mention perhaps because the Church has never completed a theological description of the Third Person. It is not surprising that in the sanctuary mural in the church of my childhood, while God the Father and the Son were drawn as male figures, the Holy Spirit was an amorphous cloudy fluff. Our metaphors for the Spirit (see chapter 5) are not anthropomorphic but elemental. "Holy Ghost" has for good reason passed nearly completely out of contemporary use, except in some linguistically archaic hymns. The Nicene Creed does explicitly call the Third Person Lord: but beyond these there is no other name for the Third Person than Holy Spirit.

The Hebrew word *ruah* denotes spirit or wind or breath, and we first meet this *ruah* of God as God's Spirit hovers like a nesting bird over the waters of creation (Genesis 1:2). God's *ruah* turns the soil into a living being (Genesis 2:7), and later God withdraws the divine Spirit from human beings so that they will not be immortal (Genesis 6:3). In the Hebrew Scriptures the spirit is an action of God that can create life or wreak destruction; the "Spirit of the Lord" is the divine impulse to conquer and survive (Judges 3:10); it is a power that allows the prophet to perform wonders (I Kings 18:12). Throughout, it remains a mysterious power, a sign of divine action that cannot be harnessed, whose movements are gratuitous, both gracious and devastating.

In the synoptics, God's Spirit is an agent of power, descending with a sign of peace at Jesus' baptism (Mark 1:10), driving Jesus into the wilderness (Mark 1:12), enabling Jesus to cast out demons (Matthew 12:28). In Paul's theology and in John's high-priestly prayer the Spirit is suddenly, newly, personified. The Spirit — in Greek, *pneuma* — "he" will come, he will teach, he will dwell (John 15:26). For John the Spirit of God is the Spirit of the resurrected Christ, as if the Third Person were the manner in which the Second Person, now at God's right hand, remains operative in the Church. Thus the word "spirit" calls us into a mingling of metaphor: the breath of creation, the force behind the judges and the prophets, the power of Jesus, the being of God present in the world today. How much we equate the Spirit of God solely with the work of Christ is the historic *filioque* controversy: Does the Spirit proceed always from the Son? For ecumenical goodwill it is becoming common to recite the Nicene Creed in its original form, which did not include the controverted phrase "and the Son," thus allowing the question to stand unanswered.

In an attempt to rectify the overwhelmingly masculine imagery for God in our tradition, some are suggesting that we call especially God the Spirit "she."[15] The Hebrew *ruah* is a feminine noun, and the Spirit's mysterious, intuitive, and nurturing qualities lead some to see the Spirit's nature as stereotypically feminine. The Spirit-she is a useful image and a helpful corrective. But we are being naive about language if we suppose that those who speak languages in which common nouns have grammatical gender actually believe in any essential sexuality inherent in the gender. A table as "she" has no sexuality or gender inclination. If when we call Spirit "she" we mean to suggest God's "feminine" characteristics, that is fine. However, the use of such Jungian archetypes that divide human characteristics into masculine and feminine is in many ways counterproductive for the women's movement: even in Jungian psychology each whole person is a balance of masculine and feminine qualities. However, if we call Spirit "she" to grant the Spirit feminine sexuality, that is unacceptable: not because we end up with a god only one-third feminine, but because gender designations further entrench a belief that "he" or "she" actually refers to something sexual in God's being.[16] Contemporary American English has natural gender: that is "he" and "she" are used to refer only to beings with actual sexuality. Thus in contemporary American English for God, Father, Son, and Holy Spirit, neither "he" nor "she" is appropriate.

We find it difficult to talk about God as person without implying sexuality. Since the Scriptures do not name the Holy Spirit with any images of anthropomorphic sexuality, we find it hard to picture the Holy Spirit, and artists resort to a bird or a puff of cloud. Sexuality is essential to humanity. Because we are frail and because we will die, we search for wholeness and try to live on in our children: thus the definition of the human being as a sexual because a mortal being. In the ancient pantheons, when immortal gods were sexual, their sexuality was quickly turned toward display of destructive power: sexuality apart from mortality made no sense. The Christian tradition has, at its theological best, always maintained that God is three persons without the sexuality and mortality essential for humanity. When the Greek theologians used the word *hypostasis*, which we translate "person," they meant something more like our word "mode" than like our twentieth-century psychological category of the "person."[17] Our asexual yet personal naming of the Holy Spirit illustrates better than does the language of "Father" and "Son" our theological sensitivity to the nature of divinity.

Because the Church has never agreed whether God acts through the word of Christ, through the power of the Spirit, both, or in what order, the one place in the liturgy evoking the Spirit remains a spot of continuing controversy. The *epiclesis*, one of the few times in the liturgy that the Spirit is mentioned, is the petition in the eucha-

ristic prayer in which we call down the power of the
Holy Spirit. The questions have been many: What does
the Spirit do? On what does the Spirit descend? Where
should this petition stand in relation to the words of
Christ in the institutional narrative? Liturgical scholars
generally agree that the origin of the *epiclesis* lies in the
Hebrew plea for the coming of the kingdom.[18] Christians
plead for the coming of God's reign by praying that the
Spirit of Christ return and remain on the present event
and on the whole people of God.

Contemporary eucharistic prayers reflect this controversy. Roman Catholic prayers ask before the *Verba* for
the Spirit to descend on the gifts; Protestant prayers tend
to follow the Eastern practice of placing the *epiclesis*
after the institutional narrative. But in either case the
prayers are similarly vague about what the Spirit does.
Send your Holy Spirit, so that *x* is accomplished: the use
of the passive voice grammatically detaches God's sending from any specific action of the Spirit. The Lima
Liturgy,[19] which provides an ecumenical compromise by
including two *epicleses*, one on the gifts before the *Verba*
and one on the people after the *Verba*, is bold in award-
ing to the Holy Spirit an active verb: the Spirit will
"transfigure" the meal. The biblical image of the transfiguration of the body of Christ provides a happy
substitution for our unsatisfactory philosophical categories. In this and in several other contemporary
eucharistic prayers, the epicletic petition is followed by a
congregational response, "*Veni Creator Spiritus*," "Come,
Holy Spirit" — a welcome innovation in the Western
eucharistic rite.

THE TRINITY: THE AARONIC BLESSING

The word "Trinity" is seldom used in direct address,
perhaps because it is too conceptual for personal speech.
It is "Father, Son, and Holy Spirit," the three names
together, that Christianity uses to name the Trinity.
Since liturgical prayer is addressed almost exclusively to
the First Person, it is uncommon for the Trinity as
Trinity to be invoked. Poets and mystics have suggested

56

metaphors for the Trinity, but no other proper names have been claimed by the tradition.

Some in the contemporary Church are challenging the continued use of the traditional naming of the Trinity because of the sexism implied.[20] Especially where artists have drawn God as one old man, one young child, and a bird, the traditional language has failed to represent the transcendent God. "To represent the God of Sabaoth (that is, the Father) on icons with a grey beard, with his only Son on his lap, and a dove between them, is exceedingly absurd and unseemly," spoke the Great Moscow Council in 1667.[21] But unfortunately in late Russian icons and throughout the Western tradition, the Trinity has been so pictured. The early icon tradition illustrates the advantages of metaphor in its practice of depicting the Trinity as the three visitors to Abraham.

The names of the Trinity come from the New Testament's admittedly incomplete descriptions of the relationship between Jesus and God. Terminology from Greek philosophy (*Progenitor*, *Logos*) has been rejected for terms of human relationship. The names of the Trinity are the names for God, centering on the mystery of Christ: that is, the Father is the father, not of us, but of the Son; the Spirit is the spirit also of the Son. Current suggestions to replace these biblical names with functional titles (Creator, Maker, Redeemer, Sustainer) are unsatisfactory. Here the Christian names of God, that is, the reality of God in relation to Christ, are rejected for functions as humans perceive them. We could then endlessly debate: Who is Creator, the First, Second, or Third Person? What about the crude phallic connotation of the title Maker? Is it appropriate to retain the metaphor of Redeemer with its archaic notion of the atonement as payment to God or to the devil? Functions of the Third Person are vague: what is a sustainer? "Sanctifier" conveys very little. "God, Christ, and the Spirit" suggest either tritheism or Arianism and skirts the issue of the relationship between God and Jesus.

Since we are given such a restricted naming of the Trinity, it is consoling that the Trinity's name scarcely appears in public worship. Some eucharistic rites begin or conclude with a trinitarian invocation or blessing; in repeating the baptism formula, we name God with these names because we live under the cross. We stand in relationship to God because of our relationship to Christ. More commonly the words of Paul are used: "The grace of our Lord Jesus Christ, the love of God, and the communion of the Holy spirit be with you all" (2 Corinthians 13:14). In this early trinitarian blessing the sexual connotations present in Father, Son, and Holy Spirit are much diminished while the mystery of the Trinity is affirmed and praised.

Martin Luther preferred the Aaronic blessing (Numbers 6:24-26).[22] It conveys the image of the Trinity with a single name. "The LORD bless you and keep you": the LORD of the burning bush blesses and keeps us. These verbs recall the mercy of God proclaimed in the Hebrew Bible. "The LORD's face shine upon you and be gracious to you": here we see the LORD in the face of Jesus Christ, recalling John's gospel that to see Jesus is to see God (John 14:9). The word "gracious" recalls the forgiveness granted us in the cross. "The LORD look upon you with favor and give you peace": we pray for *shalom*, the gift of God's Spirit, the peace given the faithful after the resurrection. The Aaronic blessing brilliantly superimposes the Johannine images of the Son and the Spirit on the Hebrew teaching of the one God YHWH. This blessing is perhaps the most religiously lively manner in which to call upon the Trinity in liturgical speech. Trinitarian doctrine is called to mind through images of creation, incarnation, and sanctification. We stand together receiving the gaze of the three-in-one eye of God. It is a good benediction.

NEW NAMES?

Because the biblical canon has never been closed, because the councils of the Church have never agreed that the last word interpreting the revelation has been spoken, some ask whether the Church might agree on new names for God, whether functional titles for the Trinity or a wholly new name, like "Mother." Will "God

the Mother" find its way into sacred speech as a name
for God?

The Christian Scriptures are those writings that
interpret the meaning of Christ by juxtaposing the
Hebrew religious tradition to the cross. What does it
mean to be a child of Abraham? What did Moses say of
redemption? Who is the man called Jesus? We look to the
books of the apostolic witness to answer these questions.
The first-century Christian writers produced both a
history of their faith and a commentary on the Hebrew
Scriptures. While the interpretation of these texts continues, orthodox Christianity is not open to new revelation.
New revelation creates the Shakers, the Mormons, those
sects with fascinating exaggerations that remain on the
fringe of the historic faith. Christianity claims that in
Christ was the complete revelation of God and that the
final, ultimate revelation of God will come at the end
time, again in Christ. We receive this apostolic tradition,
affirm it, and speak it in contemporary words.

Around this revelation of God in Christ we are given
the name of God, such as we know it. That name is
partial, subject to the maiming force of human language
and to our careless handling of divine life. Our first step
in affirming God's name must be our humble realization
that no human being can fully know the name of God or
can finally and completely call down God's mysterious
being. Before the name of Christ we kneel in faith, but
with the name of God there is always the stuttering of
Moses and Isaiah (Exodus 4:10, Isaiah 6:5). No, these are
not God's names. Yes, this is how we name God, with
these names, around the mystery of Christ. This is how
we address our prayers, trusting in the cross.

It is difficult to imagine any new name of God
arising to unite God's people. The Book of Revelation
suggests that in the end time we will finally know God's
name and will wear it on our forehead, as now we wear
the cross of the water of our baptism and the cross of the
ashes of our mortality (Revelation 22:4). Perhaps that
name will be silence, or "Mother." Until that day, however, we join at the foot of the cross in the praise of the

Church. The psalms teach us how to employ metaphor after metaphor in our praise and pleas to God. Our poets, preachers, hymnwriters, and artists ought to be more free than they are to explore new metaphors for God. "Mother" is one such metaphor that can arouse our religious imagination. The metaphors must go on. But the proper names for God are there, in the scrolls of the Torah, on the inscription over the cross, and in the writings of Paul and John. And they are there on our foreheads, in baptism.

SECOND THOUGHTS

In this chapter I talk about God's "names" as those metaphors so basic to the tradition that they can refer, "while not univocally, at least more than usually," to the deity Christians worship. Shiva and Mother Earth are different deities from the Trinity: the divine name that we employ in prayer does matter. Yet in recent polemics concerning the triune name, it is clear that some Christians use the term "God's name" with a quite technical meaning, as if God "has" "a name," revealed in certain Bible passages, a name that is analogous to the name stipulated on our birth certificates. I hope to distinguish my use of the term "divine name" from such borderline fundamentalism: biblical scholars who are not fundamentalists do not strengthen their side of controversial positions by piously citing Bible verses. We need, rather, to attend to the meaning of biblical language throughout the history of the Church to see which metaphors have become and can remain the primary language of faith.

There are many comments I could make concerning the material in this chapter. Indeed, I have written an entire book, *God beyond Gender*, dealing with some of these issues. Let me here cite a few pertinent facts about the biblical naming of God which I have learned in the past several years.

Since many of these comments touch on gender issues, let me first offer several definitions. "Sex" refers to the anatomical distinction between two versions of the species that some animals and plants require for reproduction. We call these two versions male and female. Holly trees, cats, and humans have sex. Angels do not. To confuse our conversation, the word "sex" also is used regularly as an abbreviation for sexual intercourse. "Gender," on the other hand, is a linguistic or cultural category of thought. That is, many languages organize nouns and pronouns by gender, in which male, female, and neuter gender may or may not agree with natural sexuality. In German, the noun for "girl" is neuter. American speech is gradually eliminating linguistic gender from its usage: a country is now an "it," not a "she." "Gender" also delineates cultural stereotypes, as in the idea of "feminine behavior." In Ghana, feminine behavior includes the ability to carry enormous bundles on one's head while walking long distances. I try to distinguish carefully between sex and gender. The Christian theological tradition has consistently taught that God has no sex. I also assert that God has no gender.

Concerning "name": The biblical phrase "in the name of" does not mean "here is the given name." It means rather "in the power of," "under the authority of." "Name" is used as a synecdoche, a part that stands for the whole. God's "holy arm" is a synecdoche that refers to divine power. God's "name" is a synecdoche that refers to God's being. Thus "in the name of the Father, and of the Son, and of the Holy Spirit" means not that what follows is God's name, but that the action being taken bears the power of God.

Concerning *El Shaddai:* I have learned that the root word, which refers to peaks, may have denoted the peaks of the goddess's breasts, rather than the mountain peaks of the god's domain. If this is true, its traditional rendering as "almighty" is even less fortuitous that I had previously thought.

Concerning "YHWH": There is evidence of the invocation of this divine name among tribal peoples in the eastern Sinai prior to 1300 B.C.E. Thus, similar to other biblical divine names, also this privileged name was borrowed from another religious tradition and incorporated by the Israelite people into their own religious vision. And of course the people did speak this most holy name aloud for centuries before the religious authorities restricted its use for themselves. An oral culture had to have pronounced the word in order for the tradition to be conveyed to the next generation. Some Jewish scholars now suggest that the word was onomatopoetic of deep breathing.

Concerning *Abba*: The proposal of the Aramaic scholar Joachim Jeremias, that *Abba* indicated a child's intimate address to the father, was extremely influential in mid-century among Christian theologians. In fact, Jeremias provided the scholarly support for the decision by some liturgists to translate *Deus* as Father. However, further research has cast doubt on the assertion that *Abba* was unique to Jesus, and Jeremias' precise interpretation of the word as child's speech has been challenged in several scholarly studies.

Concerning "Father": Although it is probably true that first-century Jews did not generally, perhaps ever, address God as "my father" in their communal prayer, it is absolutely true that first-century Romans, in a natural manifestation of their extremely patriarchal culture, referred to Jupiter as "Father" all of the time. One could argue that the incorporation of the title "Father" by Jews indicated not so much a revelation by Jesus of divine mercy, as a cultural adaptation of their liturgy. That is, even the religion of Jews was now reflecting the Hellenism of their environment. Thus the Church must avoid overblown claims about some Christian uniqueness to the divine title "Father." Centuries of patriarchal cultures all over the world employed the name "Father" for their primary deity.

Concerning "God": The resurgence of neo-paganism has worked to minimize feminist Christian interest in the word "Goddess" or "God/ess." Its current popular referents to either nature or the self argue against its use by Christians, who worship a deity apart from the created universe and other than the self.

Concerning the categories "masculine" and "feminine": These adjectives are both too vague to mean much and too explosive to keep around. I now say "male" or "female," if sexuality is what I am talking about. I no longer talk in a positive way about the attempt to stress "feminine characteristics" in God, for example, by calling the Spirit "she," since it is not clear to me what "feminine characteristics" are. Having learned a thing or two about both the vast variety of gender patterns in the world's current and ancient cultures and the meaning of god and goddess language in polytheisms, I minimize, rather than maximize, the differences between females and males, and I refuse to suggest that female connotes nice and male nasty.

Concerning linguistic gender: The world's languages present an astonishing array of gender systems. One of my favorites is in the language Daly, a North Australian Aboriginal dialect, which boasts nine genders: one is used for kinship and some body parts, another for other body parts, a third for male animates excluding dogs, a fourth for female animates, a fifth for dogs, and so on. Neighboring dialects of the same language can differ in their choice of which gender is used if the sex of the referents is unknown or mixed. This is to say that translation of gendered words from one linguistic system to another is an exceedingly complex proposition. It is pastorally well-intentioned but linguistically ill-informed to assert that because the Hebrew *ruah* is feminine gender, Americans should render the Spirit "she."

So here it is: the more I have learned, the less definitively I can speak on these issues.

The "name" I have most reflected on is LORD/Lord. The Church needs a way to say its Christology, that is, to apply the name of God to Jesus Christ. Yet the historic choice of "Lord," the term denoting male authority, is now controversial. Some Christians continue to defend its use. Many African-American churches use the term repeatedly in liturgical texts and hymnody as an expression of their high Christology. However, some African-American Christians reject the word as too hierarchical; many Christians are using "Lord" less than previously; and some feminist Christians reject the term totally. We must continue to search for language in which we can name Christ as God without implying that

God is male. While I do not argue that the Church needs
to purge its speech of the word "Lord," I do advocate our
finding alternative expressions. There is no question that
substitutions for LORD/Lord are being made Sunday after
Sunday throughout the land. Most replacements, however, do not pass the christological test. I have suggested
as an alternate circumlocution for YHWH "the Living
One," a phrase that aptly applies not only to God the I
AM, but also to the risen Christ. The traditional "LORD
God, through Christ our Lord" would become "the Living
God, through Christ, the Living One." Perhaps the
Aaronic blessing, which I continue to admire, can be
newly rendered. The task is this: to design a new transla-
tion that sounds three thousand years old.

Concerning the continued use of the *Gloria in
Excelsis*: Many eucharistic assemblies no longer sing the
"Glory to God" regularly. Current liturgical design tends
to condense all the material prior to the readings; many
musical settings of the Gloria are ungainly; to many
people, the hymn's structure is opaque; the use of optional canticles meets the contemporary interest in
variety; and, as well, the classic hymn is loaded with
androcentric imagery.

I continue to believe that beginning our liturgical
worship with hearty songs of praise is a good idea. I can
only hope that any replacements we choose are able to
offer as much content, present as many images, and echo
the Bible as often as does the classic *Gloria in Excelsis*. A
prominent United Methodist liturgist teaches what we
might call the Ramp-Cane Principle: A town council
decided, in deference to its residents in wheelchairs, to
ramp the corners of the sidewalks at intersections. Only
after the construction was completed did the townspeople discover that now blind persons using a cane
walked out into the traffic. We may solve one problem —
say, androcentric or incomprehensible imagery — only to
introduce another — say, unimaginative or mindless
prose.

Concerning the Spirit: I am no longer satisfied with
the minimal manner in which I dealt with the Spirit.
Dozens of newly composed hymns show evidence that

many Christians are focusing on the work of the Spirit in ways that the historic Western liturgy did not. I suggest that the word "Lord" may be replaced, for example in the exchange of peace, with the phrase "the risen Christ," but at other places, for example at the outset of the eucharistic meal, with the phrase "May the Spirit of God be with you all." The word "Spirit" is loose enough that it can sometimes connote only our perhaps high emotions, but I hope that in Christian liturgy the word "Spirit" will retain its trinitarian meaning: the Holy Spirit that Christians encounter and embody is nothing other than the Spirit of God that was in Christ and that is now manifest in the believing assembly. In all likelihood, God's Spirit is in many other places as well, but it is in the eucharistic assembly that its presence is promised to the Church.

Concerning the triune name: This is where arduous study and inspired creativity is now required. My chapter cited some of the problems with popular replacements of "Father, Son, and Holy Spirit." The increasingly popular phrase "God, Christ, and the Spirit" indicates our seriously deficient attention to the writings of the fifth-century trinitarian theologians, since the formulation suggests that God and Christ are two different beings. Indeed, any phraseology in which the three-ness overtakes the one-ness is a problem.

This issue cannot be dismissed. What needs continued work is our trinitarian theology. I am among those feminist Christians who view the Trinity as the salvation of a too-male Christology. We can take comfort for our arduous task from the fact that even Augustine wrote of the inadequacy of the name "Father, Son, Holy Spirit." Perhaps, as he suggested, we can turn to Romans 11:36, with its "from whom, through whom, and in whom," for alternate phraseology. One alternative worth our attention is Ruth Duck's naming of God as Source, Word and Spirit. Without an orthodox understanding of both the person of Christ and the place of the Spirit in the life of the Trinity, however, our attempts to offer non-gender-specific naming of God will be insufficient for Christian proclamation.

— 5 —
Metaphors for God

INVITATORY —Haps

THE FIRST PERSON: THE MORNING PSALM

Our oldest descriptions of morning prayer appoint
Psalm 95 to begin the day. Thus for 1500 years Christians have risen from bed to sing this psalm of praise to
God. Yet not for this reason alone is Psalm 95 an appropriate place to begin examination for our metaphors for
God: Psalm 95 contains several of the most significant,
most recurring metaphors for God found in the Hebrew
Scriptures. Since the God of the psalms is our God, we do
well to start here.

The psalm's main theme is the praise of Israel's God
as the God above all other gods. YHWH is called the
great *El. El* was the name of the head of the Canaanite
pantheon. In this psalm Israel claims that head god as its
own by naming *El* with the sacred name revealed to
Moses. This psalm recalls ancient mythology, before
monotheism was assumed, when there were other gods
competing with YHWH — an appropriate psalm for our
time! The psalm names our God, our *El*, with the mysterious gifted name, and claims our *El* supreme.

Verses 4-5 of the psalm picture this *El*, YHWH, as
the creator of the universe. Israel commonly called God
creator: Genesis 1 and 2, Psalm 104, and Job 38 are
examples of stories of God's creative power. In the ancient Near East, creation stories did not attempt to
answer scientific questions about origins but rather
attempted to give religious answers to our fears concerning chaos. Creation is an ordering of the chaotic void
(the *tohuwabohu* of Genesis 1:2), a garnering of the
deeps (Psalm 104:6-9), a taming of the sea monster (Job
7:12). By creating order out of chaos, God is the maker of
the universe. In God's hands the creation is held and
upheld: the psalm speaks metaphorically, as if God had

66

hands. In another example of anthropomorphism, God is likened to a potter who formed the world from the mass of matter, shaping the universe with divine wisdom and forethought.

The Canaanite *El* was also called "creator," but as was common in ancient mythologies, the creator *El* was alienated from the present world, linked with natural disasters, and experienced as inexplicable terror. In the psalms of Israel, on the other hand, the creator God is benevolent, the God who adopts and saves the people. Thus God is a good king, an approachable monarch. This cultic psalm calling the people to worship — "O come!"— demonstrates the welcome this monarch gives. Verses 6-7 suggest that God is king especially of those who are saved. The emphasis is not on the absolute monarch as much as on a fortunate people. The metaphor of shepherd appears in tandem with that of king. Shepherd was an ancient Near Eastern metaphor for the king, who with a rod beat back the enemy and with a staff rescued the fallen. In this psalm creation and salvation are held together, YHWH the God of Genesis and of Exodus, of the created universe and of the saved people.

Psalm 95 also calls God "rock." This is a fascinating and complex metaphor. We think of the rock as stability in the storm, as shade from the sun, as foundation for the edifice. But in ancient times rocks functioned as symbols of divine power, as if the rock were a concentrated form of creation. In some cults the stone was set up as a phallic symbol of divine prowess; in others the stone, hollowed out to recall the womb of the deity, was used as an altar of sacrifice. The story of Jacob's ladder gives a salvific interpretation to one such sacred stone (Genesis 28:18-19) as Jacob anoints with oil a significant stone and erects it as a pillar of God's house. In the Hebrew narrative the rock is made to give forth God's water in the desert (Exodus 17:6). It is significant that the sacred rock spouting water is located near Mount Horeb, which is called the mountain of God. The rabbis later told the story that the rock followed the Israelites around the wilderness for forty years, giving the people continuous living water. A dozen psalms use this metaphor, praising God as the rock of the people's salvation. Later legend claimed that Solomon's temple was built upon the primordial rock that marked the center of the universe. Islam's Dome of the Rock appropriated this rock as the center of its religious world.

We sing Psalm 95 as Christians. "That rock is Christ," says Paul (1 Corinthians 10:4), claiming not only that Christ is our rock but that also for the wandering Jews, the "supernatural Rock which followed them" was Christ. In Greek, "rock," *petra,* is a feminine noun. Made into a masculine form, the word becomes *petros,* the name Jesus gave the apostle Simon (Matthew 16:18). This chain of metaphors describes the faith of Peter and, by extension, of the Church appropriating Christ, the rock. The epistle of 1 Peter carries the metaphor even further. Christ is the rock, and we are stones fixed next to Christ and thus creating the house of God (I Peter 2:5). And more: Christ as the rock is also the stumbling block, the rejected stone, the scandal to trip up the religious world (1 Peter 2:7-8). For if religions in ancient times depicted the great god or goddess as a sacred rock, those religions trip over the rock at the door of Christ's tomb, the crucifixion and resurrection breaking sacred metaphor.

There are layers of meaning. For us the rock is God, and Christ, and the faith of the Church, and the scandal of the cross. Along with Thomas we acclaim the risen Christ "my Lord and my God" (John 20:28) — in the words of Psalm 9, my YHWH and my *El.* John's prologue teaches us that creation came to be through the word of God who is Christ. Medieval statues sculpted the youth Jesus in a Johannine way, holding in his hands the orb of universal power; it was only in the humanism of the Renaissance that this symbol of majesty became the child's ball. For Christ is our monarch, enthroned on a cross; Christ is our shepherd, the first of the lambs to die.

We Christians sing this psalm at the opening of the day. "Come, let us sing to the Lord," we chant to one another, using the ancient enthronement song to recall our baptism as God's newly saved people. Yet these are metaphors: the greatest *El,* the creator, the potter, the

68

king, the shepherd, the rock. God is not anything like the ancient Canaanite mythic deity. God has no hands, is not a male ruler, has no sheep, is not mere stone. But we use these metaphors to call one another to faithful worship of God, and we break the religious metaphors over the cross on our way.

[handwritten margin note: INVITATORY RIDER CONTEXT]

THE SECOND PERSON: THE *AGNUS DEI*

We have seen that Christians interpret many metaphors for God as applying also to Christ. But some metaphors are used exclusively for the Second Person. One such metaphor extremely important in the eucharistic liturgy is that of the Lamb of God.

Since about 700 when Pope Sergius I regularized its position in the liturgy, Christians have sung the *Agnus Dei*, "Lamb of God," after the eucharistic prayer at the beginning of communion. Originally the phrase from John 1:29, "Lamb of God who takes away the sin of the world," was chanted repeatedly during the fraction. Over the centuries in the West the petitions "Have mercy upon us" and "Grant us peace" were put in place and the repetitions kept to three; with the decline of the fraction, the chant became a communion song.

[handwritten margin note: peace]

[handwritten margin note: Complex] The metaphor of Christ as lamb is a complex one. Christians learn this metaphor largely from the Johannine literature.[1] John the Baptizer calls out to the crowd, "Behold, the Lamb of God, who takes away the sin of the world!" (John 1:29). Already in the Baptizer's mouth this metaphor has several referents. In the first place, standing in a tradition of apocalyptic preaching, John the Baptizer was one of the prophets who employed a complicated scheme of metaphors to talk of the end time with its punishment of evildoers and its vindication of the just. Indeed, intertestamental literature refers to an apocalyptic lamb who will conquer and destroy evil in the world. The Book of Revelation, with its thirty-some references to the conquering Christ as "a lamb standing, though it had been slain" (Revelation 5:6), relies on this apocalyptic metaphor. This lamb will conquer all evil and will vindicate the chosen ones (Revelation 17:14). In

Matthew's apocalyptic vision of the last judgment, Christ appears as the Lord of the sheep (Matthew 25:33). Thus this metaphor suggests that Christ is the one who in the end time will vanquish evil and right wrongs. It is of course strange to symbolize victory with the weak lamb. Thus the ancient metaphor is readily appropriate as a picture of Jesus dying on the cross.

Second, Luke records Philip as giving a different interpretation to the lamb metaphor (Acts 8:32-35). In this narrative, the image of the lamb of Isaiah 53 is applied to the crucified Christ. In Isaiah's song of the suffering servant, the chosen one, like a lamb, takes on himself the guilt of us, who are the other sheep. The suffering lamb is led silently to the slaughter. This metaphor suggests that Jesus is the chosen one of God, suffering yet innocent, the perfect servant. The image of Jesus as suffering servant is important in the Passion in Mark: Jesus stands mute at his trial (Mark 14:61). The chosen one bears the sin of the many other sheep. Thus in this interpretation the Lamb of God is the innocent yet suffering servant, chosen by God to be punished for us. The Torah says that a female lamb without blemish is to be slain as a sin offering for the common people and its blood placed on the altar (Leviticus 4:32). Since John says that the lamb takes away the sin of the world, this second interpretation of the lamb is significant.

Third, there is the Passover lamb. The springtime ritual of sacrificing a perfect yearling from the flock is probably an ancient one by which the nomad hopes to insure the fertility of the new flock. The ritual of smearing the blood on the doorway occurs in many religious rites as a kind of hex sign, warding off evil spirits. In Exodus these rituals are tied to the historic deliverance of the Hebrews from Egypt. The lamb is at first not thought of primarily as a sacrifice: that idea develops later with the temple cult. At first the lamb is a sign of God's deliverance and a vehicle for sacred communion: although the lamb in a sin offering was not eaten, the Passover lamb provided a joyous family festival. The Johannine account of Jesus' death relies on this metaphor. In John, Jesus dies just as the lambs are being slain

70

for the Passover meal; while on the cross, Jesus is offered wine on hyssop. Considering that hyssop is a wholly unlikely plant for use either as a pole or a sponge, John must have meant to remind us of the metaphor of the Passover lamb with its herb garnish of hyssop (John 19:28-31, Exodus 12:22). The metaphor of the Passover lamb suggests that Jesus is the one whose blood brings deliverance and whose body provides our feast. 1 Peter 1:19 recalls this image in saying that we are ransomed "with the precious blood of Christ, like that of a lamb without blemish or spot."

Such a mingling of metaphor! Christ is the conquering lamb at the cataclysmic end of time; Christ is the suffering lamb who bears the sins of the sheep; Christ is the Passover lamb whose body gives us food and whose blood seals our safety. We use this multivalent image of the lamb as we beg for mercy and plead for peace. Yet it is significant at what point in the liturgy we sing this song. Originally the chant, accompanying the breaking of the bread, signified that the bread was the Lamb of God for us, broken for our deliverance: thus the Isaiah image was stressed. If now the chant coincides with the beginning of communion, the connotation is different. As we eat this bread, we share in the meal of the lamb and are protected by the lamb's blood: this stresses the Passover image. But third, in an age when nuclear destruction haunts our future, the lamb as apocalyptic redeemer would be an appropriate metaphor to revive. Most musical settings, however, convey no apocalyptic strength or power: our liturgies would be richer if church composers knew their biblical images better. We plead for mercy and peace, and the liturgy offers us the bread and the wine as a foretaste of God's fullest mercy.

We should give this central symbol of the lamb as complete and as rich an interpretation as its complex history warrants. It is curious that in liturgical art the lamb is usually depicted sitting down, rather like a pet cat. Yet not the conquering lamb nor the suffering lamb nor the lamb consumed would look as innocuous as our pictures suggest. We cannot plead urban culture and escape this image without great loss to the Judeo-Christian metaphor of God's ways. For it is not the earthly lamb with whom we need acquaintance. A trip to the petting zoo shows only a rather dirty and stupid animal. We need rather to tell the stories of Exodus and Isaiah and Revelation and so see more of the lamb than we thought was there.

THE THIRD PERSON: *"VENI CREATOR SPIRITUS"*

In liturgical prayer the Church asks the Father to send the Spirit who will bring the blessing of Christ. The Spirit is invoked during the eucharistic prayer, at baptisms, confirmations, ordinations, and on Pentecost. The Scriptures give us few names and metaphors for the Spirit, and the ordinary of the liturgy has little reference to the Third Person. For metaphors of the Spirit we must look to hymnody, where Christian poets have always been ready to rhapsodize on this mysterious being of God.

The two most important hymns concerning the Spirit are *"Veni Creator Spiritus"* and *"Veni Sancte Spiritus."* [2] *"Veni Creator Spiritus"* is usually attributed to Radanus Maurus in the ninth century. Well known in John Cosin's seventeenth-century translation, "Come, Holy Ghost, our souls inspire," and available in many other translations, it is sung during Pentecost week and at ordinations. This hymn employs many metaphors for the Spirit: "creator," *"paraclete,"* "gift of God," "font of life," "fire of love," "unction," "finger of God," "promise of the Father," "guide." The second hymn, *"Veni Sancte Spiritus,"* is ascribed to Innocent III in the twelfth century. Called the "Golden Sequence," it is acclaimed one of the masterpieces of Latin poetry and is sung before the Gospel reading on Pentecost. It too is available in many translations, a common one being "Come, Holy Ghost, in love." In its lines, the Spirit is called "father of the poor," "giver of riches," "light," "counselor," "guest of the soul," "relief," "rest," "calm," and "solace." Many of these metaphors function to the same end: whatever our problem, the Spirit can solve it. If we are weary, the Spirit is rest. If we are mourning, the Spirit is solace.

Both poems beg the Spirit to reverse our pitiful condition — to restore our flesh, cleanse what is sordid, drench what is arid, bend what is rigid. From all manifestations of death the Spirit creates life. Neither hymn employs the metaphor of the dove.

The second stanza of *"Veni Creator Spiritus"* includes the familiar elemental metaphors for the Spirit: "fountain," "fire," and "unction." Each of these metaphors has a history in religious ritual, in biblical narrative, and in liturgical practice. Let us first consider "fountain." Many ancient shrines were located at springs, as if the fresh flowing water were a theophany, a sign of divine life. The Bible contains several stories of water as a sign of God's grace. To Hagar, dying of thirst in the desert, suddenly there comes a fountain of water (Genesis 21:19). For the Israelites in their wanderings, a rock becomes a fountain (Numbers 20:11). Jesus suggests to the Samaritan woman that from him springs forth living water (John 4:14): Christ is the fountain. Christian ritual has located its fountain in baptism, and we talk of this font as the washing in the Holy Spirit. In this fountain we receive the Spirit of Christ, the gift of divine life.

"Fire" is a second elemental metaphor for the Spirit. Fire appeared to Moses in the burning bush (Exodus 3:2); the pillar of fire guided the people of Israel through the wilderness (Exodus 13:21); a holy fire covered the top of Mount Sinai (Exodus 19:18); the fire descended to consume Elijah's sacrifice (1 Kings 18:38). John the Baptizer proclaimed that Christ will baptize with the Holy Spirit and with fire (Matthew 3:11); and so at Pentecost the sign of the indwelling of the Spirit of Christ is tongues as of fire (Acts 2:3). Christianity sees God not as Zeus, who punished Prometheus for giving the sacred power of fire to mortals, but as a gracious God, whose constant gift of life is likened to fire. Fire is an image of uncontainable power, a symbol of purification through devastation. Fire gives us heat and food only as it burns up other life. Fire cannot be held; it constantly moves; surrounded by brilliant yellows and oranges, its center is black. We signify the death and resurrection of Easter by lighting a fire at the opening of the Easter Vigil, and we remind children of their baptism into the Spirit by giving them a candle alive with the fire of God.

The Spirit is also called "unction," the holy anointing. In the desert, oil is a sign of life for dry limbs; in ancient religious ritual, it is a symbol of divine favor bestowed. In Israel, oil was the sign of the power of God marking the heads of priests, kings, and prophets. "Messiah" means "the anointed one": the anointing by the Spirit makes us one with the anointed one, the Messiah Jesus. Still today monarchs are anointed for their reign, and after baptism children are anointed with scented oil, chrism, as a sign of their unity with Christ, the anointed one. Yet oil is not only a sign of authority: we recall the woman who anointed Jesus beforehand for his burial (Mark 14:8). Thus oil as the seal of monarchy mingles with oil as the lubricant for the corpse; so are we, in the Spirit, anointed to reign and to die. "It is God who establishes us with you in Christ and has anointed you," Paul writes (2 Corinthians 1:21); God's seal has been placed upon us, and the Spirit is in our hearts as a guarantee. The divine unction, the seal of our anointing, is the Spirit. It is evident that the elements with which we picture the Spirit are the materials of our sacraments and rituals. The breath of exorcism, blowing out the evil spirit and blowing in holiness; the water of baptism; the fire of Easter; the unction of anointing — these objects of our ritual convey the life of the divine Spirit in our midst.

The poet of *"Veni Creator Spiritus"* does not try to capture in Latin the complex Johannine metaphor of the *Paraclete*, but simply transliterates the Greek word. Many scholars agree that this rare anthropomorphic metaphor for the Spirit is best transliterated and its meaning taught, since none of the possible translations — advocate, mediator, spokesperson, counselor, comforter, witness, helper — contains enough of John's meanings. The *Paraclete* is the divine Spirit of Jesus, which will live on in the Church after the apostles die off. The *Paraclete* will come to us, who were not direct witnesses of the resurrection, so that through this Spirit we too can see the risen Lord. The *Paraclete* is our possessing of the Spirit of Christ.

VERBS AS METAPHORS: *"VENI SANCTE SPIRITUS"*

The classic hymns to the Holy Spirit keep alive for Christianity the Hebrew pattern of describing God with verbs. Usually we think of metaphors as nouns, but the God of the Hebrews is a God who acts, and many kinds of verbs are used of God. The name of God revealed to Moses is itself a verbal form, an open verb of being. Psalm 104 describes God as creator with verbs like "cover," "stretch," "lay," "make," "set," "cause." Psalms 105 and 106 recount all the deeds of God in Israel's history by a long catalogue of verbs. Psalm 107 makes a poem out of archetypal saving deeds of God, who satisfies the hungry, shatters bronze doors, and stills storms. Psalm 136 is an antiphonal hymn of one verb after another. In Psalm 18 the verbs are more clearly metaphorical: God thunders, belches smoke, trains the foot soldier. The *Magnificat,* sung at evening prayer for centuries, follows this pattern of praise. At the close of the day God is praised for all God has done: the canticle is in the main a list of verbs. In *"Veni Creator Spiritus"* and *"Veni Sancte Spiritus,"* the activity of God is described with many verbs: God visits, fills, gives, restores, repels, washes, wets, rules, foments, enlivens, heals.

Our interpretive skills must work more quickly when the metaphor is a verb instead of a noun. In the space of a single word we are to get behind the now-dead metaphor to the original image implied by the verb. The verb "mold" implies a potter carefully crafting mud into pots on the wheel. Six such verb metaphors line up in the astonishing fourth stanza of *"Veni Sancte Spiritus"*:

> Lava quod est soridum,
> Riga quod est aridium,
> Rege quod est devium.
> Fove quod est languidium,
> Flecte quod est rigidium,
> Sana quod est saucium.

Clean what is filthy, we say, as if God were a washer-woman scrubbing away, up to the elbows in suds, and we the dirty selves run roughly, lovingly, over the board of the cross. Bend what is rigid, we ask, as if God's Spirit were a masseuse stroking the pain out of stiff muscles, as if God's Spirit were an archer forming a bow from a stout branch. The advantage of verbs as metaphors is that they tend not to inspire incompetent artists to plague us with silly depictions of God. But the disadvantage is that they go by so quickly that we scarcely have time to recall the implied metaphor.

Yet the verbs are essential to our Christian faith. Philosophical systems describe God with logically appropriate adjectives: God is eternal, unchangeable, omnipotent, omniscient. But the Judeo-Christian God is not one who sits idly by watching us choose sensible adjectives. Our God is one who acts in strange and wonderful ways. We ascribe to God the credit for all benevolent action that surrounds us. If the world receives rain, we praise God for the pouring. If we are healed of illness, we praise God for the nursing. If in the end we see God, we praise the one who unmasks divinity and shows us the face of Jesus.

FEMININE METAPHORS

Voluminous literature has been written on the subject of the excessive dominance in our tradition of masculine metaphors for God. Some scholars, urging a radical revisionist history, recast the entire Judeo-Christian tradition so that images for God are more sexually equitable.[3] Other scholars conclude that the masculine bias has so influenced the fundamental development of the tradition that even the meaning behind the metaphor must be rejected.[4] Still others maintain that while the tradition has been incorrigibly sexist, there are data in the Scriptures[5] and in the tradition[6] that allow us to continue on in a more enlightened vein. This issue of gender-specific language for God reminds us again of the NO of our critical inquiry, for despite our metaphoric language, God is neither masculine nor feminine.

76

never
DIRECT

It would be consoling were it possible for us to have
direct access to God. We wish to be released from the
limitations of our human culture. Yet our speech is mere
human speech, combining our culture's inadequate
categories and our language's insufficient vocabulary. We
cannot act surprised or chagrined when in a religion of
incarnation the divine vision is diminished by the speech
of the receiving culture. Yes, the speech of our tradition
was regrettably sexist, and as we move closer both to the
rabbis' assertion that God is beyond sexuality and to
Paul's ideal that in Christ there is no sexual dominance
(Galatians 3:28), we cannot defend or maintain the
sexism of our past. No more can we maintain aggressive
warfare because the psalms speak of God as the general
of our advancing troops. But in spite of the inadequacy of
the male-dominated speech, the sacred has been a vehicle
of God's grace and mercy to humankind. Although
"king" is not the last word on divine being, and we ought
these days to render the word "Sovereign," the royal
metaphor has conveyed God's benevolence and strength
to those in need, and it has drawn us Christians into the
paradox of the cross.

Our task is twofold. One is to free up the traditional
metaphors to speak their own riches. A shepherd is not
necessarily male: Rachel and countless Bedouin young
women before and since were shepherds. A potter is not
necessarily a man. The Passover called for a male lamb; a
sin offering, a female lamb. God's Spirit as a fountain of
living water employs a classic Jungian feminine arche-
type, God as a womb of embryonic waters, birthing us
into life. So it is that some baptismal fonts were shaped
to resemble wombs, nourishing us to eternal life. The
verb for the Spirit's hovering over the waters of creation
(Genesis 1:2) is the same verb used of a nesting mother
bird. We are called to more creative exposition of scriptural images. The metaphors that have enslaved women
in the past can be turned to signify God's freedom.

The second task is to incorporate into our liturgy
more feminine metaphors. Attention to the psalms when
creatively translated inspires us to a plethora of metaphor.[7] Newly composed hymnody can draw on feminine

imagery.[8] Our churches and our catechetical material must be purged of "pictures" of God as an old man. We can revive the image of Sophia, the holy wisdom of God. Liturgical roles can be assigned in such a way that our symbolization of the reign of God does not imply that men are the dominant sex. Daily prayer provides occasion to read again the mystics who are bold with objectifying and feminizing metaphors. In all this we do well to avoid a gender trap that assumes that masculine imagery connotes authority and mastery while feminine imagery connotes service and passivity. The liberation of women is not served by balancing male-dominance speech with female-nurturing speech. Not only is there Jochebed, protecting her infant Moses, there is also Queen Esther, saving her whole people Israel. Not only is there the apostle Paul, there is the thief on the cross. Simple-minded gender classification for symbols makes them even more restrictive than the human experience they are meant to contain.

There is, finally, the massive task of rendering the historic liturgy in appropriate contemporary American English, in which, with its abandonment of grammatical gender, God ought not be called "he."[9] In contemporary American English, gender-specific pronouns are used only for nouns of definite sex. No more is a student "he" and a ship "she." This change in the pronoun system has rendered our language more equitable, but also, for a time, somewhat awkward. This task of retranslation implies not an afternoon of substituting the word "God" for "he," but a several-decade effort to discover the vernacular way to declare the liberating gospel. The sounds will be strange to our ears. That is nothing new, for Christianity has always spoken old words in new ways, reforming the language of revelation through its vision of the cross. Those who draft liturgies and translate the Bible are at least acknowledging that masculine pronouns ought not be used for God, but few have offered in their published material a sound suggestion as to how to implement this goal. The work will not be easy: sacred speech is not self-evident. But our vision of God is at stake: it is worth the effort.

SECOND THOUGHTS

Much of my life's work has been dedicated to acti-
vating people's reception of metaphor. My chapter
illustrates how to trace the meaning of liturgical metaphor through the Bible. My recent work has extended the
inquiry, to include study of religions and cultures prior
to and outside biblical times, for I am now interested also
in how the Jewish and Christian traditions borrowed and
adapted symbolic speech from other religious systems,
and how we either reiterated other religions' symbols or
radically altered them. For example, how much of YHWH
was *El*? What can archeological examination of sacred
stones teach us about God as Rock? What is the difference between Father Jupiter and Father in the Trinity?
While the Bible is Christians' chief source of the meaning of liturgical metaphor, the Bible does not stand in
isolation, its imagery beamed down from above. Rather,
its metaphors echo those of other religions and neighboring cultures, and the more we know of all this, the better.

I have developed what I call the Trinity Test for
Christian divine metaphors. One sees an early version of
it in my interpretation of God as "Rock." When we think
of rock as a symbol of creation, rock as Christ, and rock
as the stones of the Church, we have taken the image
"rock" through the three interpretive points of the
Trinity. The psalms call God "shepherd;" the gospels
refer to Christ as the good shepherd; and inspired by the
Spirit, we in the Church are shepherds to one another.
The Trinity Test helps christianize the countless divine
metaphors in and outside of the Bible, for it moves
archetypal divine imagery through Christology and into a
doctrine of the Spirit in the church.

The Trinity Test keeps divine imagery from floating
disembodied in the sky, remaining nailed to the cross or
referring only to nature or to ourselves. The Trinity Test
works to bring our language, and us, into the life of the
triune God. Certainly, some names and metaphors apply
more fully to one than to all three aspects of the triune

God. But the Trinity Test keeps me aware, makes me probe trinitarianly. For example, the Bible applies the image of creator not only to the first, but to all three persons of the Trinity: see Revelation 4:11, Colossians 1:16, and Job 33:4. The triune God, rather than one face of God, creates. (Thus one of the problems with "Creator, Redeemer, Sustainer.")

Concerning female metaphors: Since I wrote *Christ in Sacred Speech*, study of, experimentation about, and adoption of female metaphors for God have been extensive in world Christianity. For many Christians, the question is no longer whether, but in which contexts and how often the Church can or should incorporate female imagery. When I was a graduate student, consideration of God as "mother" in Lutheran liturgical prayer was an acceptable topic for a scholarly inquiry; now, twenty-five years later, a recent Lutheran hymnbook includes Jean Janzen's "Mothering God," which applies the metaphor of mother to each aspect of the Trinity. "Sophia" is finding its way into some worship texts. Some assemblies are replacing the line "The word of the Lord," that nearly universal phrase with which lectors conclude a Bible reading, with the phrase, "Holy Wisdom, Holy Word." Australian Christians are discussing whether God can be imaged as the Rainbow Serpent, the female creative spirit of the Aboriginal peoples. Some preachers are capable of referring to female anatomy, to God's breasts and womb — although I wonder why, just as in art museums, the female body is more available for public contemplation than is the male's. When I despair over the massive reforms still required within the androcentric Church, I am made hopeful by the considerable changes that have already been wrought in the last generation.

However, the task before us in monumental. And — I am no Pollyanna — all is not at present glorious. It is true that many Christians, both in this country and around the world, have not seen the gospel in female imagery, and, for whatever reasons resistant to change, they glorify androcentric language, defending the tradition with narrow and sometimes ignorant claims. In some areas of the Church, a great gulf is becoming fixed between those Christians who use solely historic liturgical metaphors and those who replace all male imagery with female images. Sometimes this gap separates male Christians from female Christians, or ecclesiastically loyal persons from those who dismiss traditional structures. In such cases, metaphors for God, whether venerable or innovative, can become the clubs we use to beat up on each other. The words in our prayers are hand grenades flung across the pews.

For here is the complicating truth: what is a grace-filled metaphor for one believer may be a noose for another. While some people reject the image of judge as patriarchal and hierarchical, other Christians, oppressed by systems of injustice, are waiting eagerly for a Divine Deborah to sit under the palm tree and judge the land in righteousness. Indeed, the Christmas psalm, 96, claims that the trees are singing for joy at the arrival of the Judge. I am sure that "Father" speaks grace to some believers more than "Mother" does.

I urge: always open it up, open it up. Open up the Bible, to see what the images mean. Open up the tradition, and find there Christian riches long forgotten, religious jewels locked up in dusty chests. Open up other religions and cultures, to compare, to contrast, to borrow, yes, also to criticize and to reject. Open up the memories of the conservative grandparents, for whom the traditional imagery conveyed mercy. Open up the creativity of the newfashioned writers, who can share with others fresh metaphors of mercy. Open it up, open it up. By the power of the Spirit, life, not death, will enter and grow.

O word
openness not
orthodoxy
— must have with
originality

Sacred Speech about Time

CHRISTIAN TIME

precision

The contemporary Western world heeds the clock more than did any previous civilization. Trains running on the hour, workers punching in on timeclocks, television programs beginning on the hour, clocks everywhere: life is measured out and organized by the sixty minutes of the hour. Digital clocks now on wrists and walls make us more conscious of the passing minutes; the frenetic among us note even the seconds. Prairie people or farmers of a century past would not, as we do, count the individual passing minutes. The hour is a hold with which society binds its diverse members. Western churches have capitulated: services on the hour last an hour. *ATOMIC CLOCKS*

For Christians, however, there is a radically different hour, the "hour" of salvation. In the synoptics, Jesus' hour is the time of the Passion (Mark 14:35, 41), and in John the hour becomes a metaphor for the entire salvific event of Holy Week (John 12:23). Christ's passion, his ascent on the cross, and his ascent to his Father are his hour. His hour of death becomes our hour of life. This hour is both actual clock time — we try to discover the precise dating of the crucifixion, we re-create the chronology of those days — and it is archetypal salvific time, an hour that, because it changes all time, stands above all regular hours. All hours are now altered because of the hour of Christ's Passion, all secular hours redeemed by the hour of which John writes.

The word "day" is another christologically significant term. The prophets used the phrase "the day of the Lord" to describe that great and final day, an actual day in the real future in which God would finally vindicate the righteous by destroying Israel's enemies. The LORD's day is coming, writes Isaiah (2:12), and the chapter proceeds, "In that day . . ." Despite the oppression in the present, on that great day of the LORD all wrongs would be put right. Paul and the synoptics continue to anticipate that great day. By this phrase the primitive Church meant the eschaton, the final coming of the Messiah, at which time the whole world would attest to God's reign on earth (1 Corinthians 1:8). But as we have grown to expect, the Johannine writings suggest a further step. The writer of the Apocalypse has his vision "on the Lord's day" (Revelation 1:10). The genitive "of the LORD" has become an adjective, "lordly," or "lordlike." The early Church uses "the Lord's day" to denote the day of worship,[1] the weekly time in which the resurrection is celebrated, the day in which, because of Christ, the enemy has already been vanquished and the new age begun. In calling the weekly day of worship by a name so close to "the day of the LORD," Christians have yet again altered Jewish religious language by juxtaposing tradition with the cross. The early Church also called the first day of the week the eighth day, the day of completion of the old order and the inauguration of the new. Images of creation, resurrection, and the eschaton mingle in our praise of the Son of God on Sunday, the day of the sun god.

Mircea Eliade talks of sacred time as *in illo tempore*, "at that time," as time outside time, sacred time radically separate from secular time, in which by mystical reentry into mythical time the present inexorable walk toward death is stayed.[2] *In illo tempore*, says Eliade, is mythological time thrust into the present, turning the present into other than normal time; it is a re-creation of the primordial time of the gods before time began. Some Christian traditions have benefited from this idea of sacred time as extraordinary mystery.[3] It is said that John Chrysostom exclaimed, "What care I where heaven is, when in the liturgy I am in heaven!"

But Eliade's phrase *in illo tempore* comes from the Latin liturgy where it introduced the reading of the gospel and meant precisely the opposite of mythological time. "At that time" Jesus did this, says the lector, grounding the reading in the chronological details of the historic life of Jesus. In liturgical time Christians do not escape the present hour. The assembly is not transported to a mythical time before time, mystically entering a time better than the present. In Christian sacred time this hour is sanctified by "the hour," this Lord's day becoming the day of the LORD. This hour, 10 o'clock Sunday morning, is the time of God's revelation because of the hour of Jesus' Passion, death, and resurrection. The paschal mystery hallows the secular hour. The day we anticipate, the final day of the LORD, is also a specific day in the future, not outside time, but the beginning of a new time in God.

THE LORD'S DAY: THE SUNDAY PREFACE

The primary unit of time for Christians is the Lord's Day. The primitive Church formed itself around this weekly celebration of Christ's resurrection. One welcome ingredient of the emerging ecumenical liturgical consensus is a return for all of Christendom to the weekly Eucharist on the Lord's Day: Protestants are regaining weekly communion, and Roman Catholics are finding ways to restore the primacy of the Sunday celebration. While Christians need not fret over the loss of Sunday as Sabbath, we must cooperate with renewed rigor to retain Sunday as the Lord's Day, the day redeemed by the resurrection.

The word "Sunday" calls for our attention.[4] It is speculated that a weekly calendar arose prehistorically to assist in marketing agricultural produce; but early on in some cultures the week stood in relation to a religious holy day. In accord with ancient astrological belief that each of the seven planets had dominion over one day of the week, the Romans named the first day for the sun, thought to be the closest planet. Already the apostolic fathers made happy use of the name *dies solis* in teaching about Sunday. Justin Martyr wrote, "We all assemble together on Sun-day, because it is the first day, on which God, having transformed the darkness and matter, made the world; and Jesus Christ our Saviour rose from the dead the same day."[5] Jerome talks of willingly accepting the name *dies solis,* for "on this day the light of the world, the sun of justice, arose."[6] Christians' use of the sun's day was heightened when in the fourth century the birthday of Jesus was celebrated on the winter solstice, a Roman holiday commemorating the return of the unconquerable sun god.[7] Although Anglo-Saxon substituted some Norse divinities for the Roman (Woden for Mercury, Thor for Jupiter, Frigg for Venus), we retained the sun's day, and liturgical catechesis could make more of this happy coincidence than we usually do.

One indication that the contemporary Church is restoring the primacy of Sunday is the recent adoption of a proper preface for Sunday. In the past, special prefaces were appointed only for festivals and for seasons. But an ordinary Sunday is, after all, the Lord's Day, and central to our liturgical understanding. Thus, the *Book of Common Prayer* employs the words "who on the first day of the week overcame death and the grave, and by his glorious resurrection opened to us the way of everlasting life. Therefore . . ." The *Lutheran Book of Worship* has an almost identical preface, changing "on the first day" to "on this day." The Roman sacramentary offers eight Sunday prefaces; the first one begins with the words "Through his cross and resurrection he freed us from sin and death" and goes on to quote 1 Peter 2:9, thus incorporating imagery of light.

In these Sunday prefaces the resurrection of God's Son is hailed as the victory over our death and the beginning of our life. Our assembly on this Lord's Day springs us from darkness into the light of the sun. God created light on the first day; Christ arose on the first day; John writes that the disciples received the Holy Spirit on the first day. We are caught up with the visionary of the apocalpyse on this Lord's Day to praise God with all the saints and angels, as we join with the heavenly host singing, "Holy, Holy, Holy" (Revelation 4:8). This is the rich mingling of images that can help us interpret our weekly celebration of the Lord's Day.

THE YEAR: THE *EXSULTET*

The paschal mystery of the death and resurrection of Christ establishes not only the Christian week but also the Christian year. Most religions and cultures celebrate the turn of the year, agriculturally, astrologically, or politically. The early Christians retained the Jewish springtime holy day, Passover, as their celebration of the transfer from death to life, a watching for the coming of the Lord. Paul equates the slain Christ with the Passover lamb and our new life with matzo (1 Corinthians 5:7-8). But as in everything Christians had to alter Jewish practice in light of the mystery of Christ. By the second century the Christian *pascha* had become an annual celebration of the resurrection of the Lord. Jewish roots are not forgotten: not only is the date for Western Easter set in relationship to Passover, but throughout the sacred Triduum — Maundy Thursday, Good Friday, and Easter Eve — the metaphors proclaiming Christ's resurrection are grounded in the experience of Israel. It would take a whole book to trace all the mingled metaphors of the Triduum. Here we will concentrate only on the Vigil of Easter Eve, especially on the great proclamation of Easter, the *Exsultet*.[8]

The Easter Vigil has its roots in the second century, and originally, as the name suggests, lasted all night, providing a metaphoric vigil first awaiting Passover and later awaiting the resurrection. After centuries of development, misuse, and disuse, the Vigil is returning, with its four services of Light, Lessons, Baptism, and Eucharist. The best way for anthropologists to study what Christians mean by liturgy would be to attend a fine Vigil, for here we see *par excellence* what liturgy is. Way back then Jesus died and rose; and here we are, the present Church, awaiting the final victory: what are we to do in the meantime? We light God's lamp in the world's darkness, listen to the great stories of the faith, baptize and anoint new members, and share in the holy meal, so that our life in the world, outside these events, is renewed. This is what it means to be the Church, and this is what constitutes the Vigil, the queen and mother of all Christian liturgy.

The Vigil begins, preferably, outside in darkness. A light is struck. We do not use some flimsy cardboard match: this is the new fire of the new year, replacing those great bonfires lit on the countryside to call Woden down to bless the crops. But far from our being punished by Zeus for stealing sacred fire, we share the fire of God's self, the light of Christ. Some ancient paschal candles were six feet tall, the better to be a sign of the one who lighted the world. The twenty-foot paschal candlestands in European cathedrals stir us with a sense of what lighting such a candle would have been like. The candle is marked with the cross of Christ, the *alpha* and *omega* of all time, and the four digits of the calendar year; for Christian sacred time is always this year redeemed by the eternity of God. Five nails with incense mark the cross, for this great light heals us only after the wounds of death. Following this pillar of fire, we process into the church and share out its flame, chanting our thanks for the light of Christ. And now we are ready to hear what is perhaps the greatest liturgical text of all Christendom. The *Exsultet* comes to us from the late fourth century, and each contemporary service book offers its own translation of this classic text.

"Rejoice now, all heavenly choirs of angels," begins the *Lutheran Book of Worship*'s translation. Happily English affords us the word "rejoice" to translate *exsultet;* with its call to happiness, a common yet noble word, we begin the exuberant chant of praise. We call the choirs of angels to sing with us, those angels who sang at Jesus' birth (Luke 2:14), who announced the resurrection (Luke 24:4), and who surround the heavenly throne with their praise (Revelation 7:11). Ancient Mesopotamian angels carried out the will of the gods and guarded the holy places, but in Christian speech these messengers of God themselves become agents of praise to God, as if the will of God for all created things is the praise of God. Christ is the enthroned king, and royal imagery is invoked: "Sound the trumpet of salvation!" Here again the Jewish image gets turned to Christ. In the Old Testament a trumpet called the people into their solemn assemblies (Exodus 19:13), and in the Book of Revelation the opening of heaven is signaled by the sound of the trumpet (Revelation 4:1). The old cultic trumpet now acclaims Jesus who as the Messiah brings in the victorious new age.

The image of light is invoked in a marvelously metaphoric way. The earth is stunned by the excessive brilliance of light; darkness "has been banished from all the world"; the church is drenched with whiteness; the congregation stands in the clarity of the light. But recall that the cantor sings by the single flame in the pitch dark! So Easter at the Vigil calls forth more faith than Easter on Sunday morning. We gather at night to laud the brilliance of the single candle of the resurrection, appearances to the contrary notwithstanding. The candle is a metaphor, our holding it high a paradoxical sign of our faith in Christ's brilliant but still unseen resurrection.

We call ourselves "O mother Church." Many Christians, in attempting to rectify the overwhelming and oppressive masculine imagery for God in the tradition, urge that just as God ought not be construed as masculine, the Church ought not be construed as feminine.[9] However, we must be able to renovate sexually based metaphors rather than discarding them altogether. The sexual metaphors can be sexist, with masculine imagery connoting power and ownership, both seen as good, and feminine imagery connoting passivity and obedience, seen as bad. As such, the metaphors are meager and even socially destructive. But this need not be. The feminine metaphors can connote creative strength. As our mother, the Church nourishes us in her womb, bears us from baptismal waters, feeds us on divine milk, and embraces us even beyond death. A mother bearing a child to life is hardly passive but rather suggests the archetypal fecundity that is the might of God. The ancient rubrics remind the presider to spill some wax from the candle into the baptismal waters. Let us hope we can enjoy the sexual symbolism of the sperm of the phallic pillar impregnating the vibrant womb of the font, that life may thrive.

"Join with me," the cantor chants. As always in the Christian assembly the presider prays the prayers of the whole people. There is no need for congregational unison prayer if the presider's prayer genuinely joins the people into one prayer. To show that we all join with the prayer of the one, we repeat the ancient dialogue of praise. "It is indeed right," responds the cantor, and so begins the main body of the *Exsultet* in which metaphor after metaphor is offered to describe the holy night and its liturgical actions. This poem gives us the images of our faith — not the data of our doctrine but the metaphors for the meaning of our baptism into the paschal mystery. "This is the night," repeats the song: this night, Easter, this Easter, Christ, this year. Again, "This is the night," the present not escaped but reconstituted in Christ.

First we recall the Garden of Eden (Genesis 3). The debt of Adam is repaid, the "necessary sin," "the happy fault" is erased. Already Paul uses the Hebrew notion that through sin God is affronted and must be assuaged (Ephesians 2:13-16). As in the medieval Christmas carol, "Blessed be the day that the apple taken was,/ There we now singen, Deo Gratias."[10] Instead of Adam's death, in place of our death, we are given the death of Christ. We sing out the paradox that since salvation is so wonderful, it is better to have sinned and been saved than never to have sinned at all.

A second image is one of redemption. The blood of Christ buys our freedom, blood for blood, life for life. Later the poem exclaims that the slave is redeemed by the Son; thus the metaphor of our unworthiness before God's grace is intensified. The imagery of our slavery leads to the story of Israel's slavery and the blood of the lamb which effected its release. And so we are brought circuitously to the Passover metaphor. Christ is the lamb, his blood marks our door (Exodus 12:13). In the metaphoric excess characteristic of this text, by Christ's blood "the doorposts of the faithful are made holy." Holy doorposts? This is one way to imagine the lintels of our church buildings, doorways sanctified by the wine served therein. We recall also the philacteries of Orthodox Jews, the word of God making holy the doorposts of the mind.

We go from Eden and Egypt to the Red Sea (Exodus 14). This night we cross the Red Sea and escape the advancing armies. Before us is the font, water for the rescue of the catechumens among us. Into the desert we go, as the candle is likened to the pillar of fire which led the people of Israel in their wanderings (Exodus 13:21). We come to the ministry of Jesus and his healings, for also in this night "all who believe in Christ" are rescued and renewed and restored. All the way to hades we go, for on this night Christ burst the chains of death (1 Peter 3:18-19). Hades is the end of the road; along with Adam and Moses and all humankind Jesus is chained by death. But the power of God bursts the chains, just as the angel causes the chains to fall off the imprisoned Peter (Acts 12:7). We recall the Eastern icons of the Harrowing of Hell, Christ rising in triumph from his chains and pulling up with him Adam and Eve.

The cantor now uses the ancient language of sacrifice, "this sacrifice of praise," "the solemn offering of the candle." Hundreds of years of quarreling over the metaphor of sacrifice are finally beginning to abate,[11] although with the Book of Hebrews as guide, it is astonishing how far afield the argument got. The pattern is familiar. What was prehistorically actual sacrifice becomes for Jews both ritual action and theological metaphor. The lambs sacrificed for sin are a sign of confession. Later the prophets, seeing the sacrificial language literally believed, urge an ethical dimension: first confess sin and do justice, then offer the bullocks. Early Christians take the Hebrew metaphor and break it on the cross. The crucifixion is the sacrifice, we say metaphorically. The crucifixion is actually an execution, but we use the strange word to say the new thing: God views this execution as if it were the archetypal sacrifice (Hebrews 7:27). The mosaics at Ravenna remind us of this metaphoric character of the term "sacrifice." At San Vitale above the table on which are placed the loaf and the cup are mosaic depictions of Abel's gift of a lamb, Abraham's offering of Isaac, and Melchizedek's presentation of bread and wine. Melchizedek's gift is in no way a literal sacrifice, yet it is used to depict our sacrifice of the Eucharist. In the *Exsultet* the offering is the candle. It is an offering but not an offering; our sacrifice is praise, a sacrifice but not a sacrifice. YES, NO, but finally YES.

Several more metaphors come. We hear the mythological idea that just as heaven and earth mated to produce life, so the human and the divine have been wed this night. (Recall the spilling of the candle wax into the water.) The bees are praised for creating the wax. Bees in the ancient world were a sign of the feminine goddess and of woman's inexplicable fertility. In medieval times the bee came to signify the virgin Mary, whose chastity carries to us the sweetness of Christ. Perhaps this is how the bees made it into the *Exsultet*! The final metaphor merges this candle with the stars of heaven, and especially with the morning star, the bright star seen in the east before sunrise. This candle, both here and in the farthest heaven, is like Christ who before the eschaton is already risen in the sky.

The throne of God, the brilliance of light, mother Church, the sin of Adam, the paschal lamb, the Red Sea, the ministry of Jesus, the harrowing of hell, the slave trade, the ancient sacrifice, the mother bee, the marriage of heaven and earth, the morning star: the *Exsultet* is a mingling of metaphors called to name the Christian mystery. After hearing this chant we are ready to listen to the seminal stories of the faith: creation, the flood, the sacrifice of Isaac, the crossing of the Red Sea, the song of Miriam, the song of the vineyard, the call to the feast, the valley of the dry bones, the three men in the fiery furnace. The *Exsultet* shows us how liturgy works: not systematic theology (although we are reminded of Anselm's theory of atonement); not private poetry (all these images are communal and ancient); but metaphoric rhetoric, the images of the past turned upon Christ, identifying our present and compelling our future. The extravagance of liturgy transforms us from a mundane life in the present hour to a sanctified life in this hour of God. How could we even think of missing the Easter Vigil?

THE DAY: THE *NUNC DIMITTIS*

Observant Jews of Jesus' day engaged in prayer three times daily. The early Christians maintained this pattern and so dedicated the day to God. The full medieval monastic office with its eight daily services of psalmody and prayer has been reformed back to the more accessible pattern of prayer at morning, noon, evening, and night.[12] Christians mark these times of day with reference to Christ, the phenomenon of the sun's light providing a continuing metaphor for Christ. The light of Sunday and the light of the paschal Vigil is also the light of each day. Using the natural image of light helps us view the pattern of the entire universe as a metaphor for our salvation. What we celebrate paradoxically at the Vigil with a single candle in the darkness we can observe more naturally in daily prayer: our waking life corresponds to the cycle of light, just as our spiritual life awakens in the light of Christ. We sleep at night, a type of death, awaiting the final morning of the eschaton. We keep the day in Christ.

The prayer offices refer to the time of day in relation to Christ. In morning prayer we sing the canticle of Zechariah, the song of the old man at the birth of John the Baptizer (Luke 1:68-79). Luke likens the coming of the Messiah to the day's dawning. According to the translation in the *Lutheran Book of Worship*,

> In the tender compassion of our God,
> the dawn from on high shall break upon us,
> to shine on those who dwell in darkness and the
>   shadow of death,
> to guide our feet into the way of peace.

Because of Christ our way is light. Evening prayer allows us the ancient ritual of *Lucernarium*, at which the light of Christ is called down on the world and the Church. The classic evening hymn, the *Phos Hilaron*, continues the reference to the day's cycle of light and dark:

> We have come to the setting of the sun,
> and we look to the evening light.

That evening light is the "joyous light of glory of the immortal Father," who is Jesus Christ. The evening psalm, Psalm 141, likens our uplifted hands to the ancient sacrifice practiced at nightfall.

From the fourth century the song of Simeon has been part of the Church's evening prayer. Most service orders now appoint it for compline, the short prayer at bedtime. After the confession, the psalm, and the short lesson, we sing with Simeon (Luke 2:29-32). Mary and Joseph have brought Jesus to the temple for his presentation. Presumably the original ceremony bought back the firstborn male from sacrifice to God with the offerings prescribed by law (Numbers 18:15). But Luke shows that around Jesus the Jewish symbols are changing shape and purpose, for even before the ritual occurs, the old man Simeon praises the child as the coming Messiah and the old woman Anna sings of God's redemption in the infant. Jesus is not redeemed from God but is the redeemer of us all.

The antiphon for the canticle is itself interesting:

Guide us waking, O Lord, and guard us sleeping,
that awake we may watch with Christ
and asleep we may rest in peace.

Awake or asleep we entrust ourselves to God: God will not sleep. The story of Jesus' agony in Gethsemane gives us the image of watching with Christ in prayer (Mark 14:37), and the phrase "Rest in peace" reminds us that our coming sleep is like death and our death only a sleep in Christ.

The canticle itself, the *Nunc Dimittis*, is only three verses long, six phrases in characteristic Hebrew poetic form, each line made of two complementary phrases. Luke tells us that Simeon has been awaiting God's salvation for Israel. The song is pertinent still to us who await the day when God's salvation is acclaimed by all the world. But Simeon sings as if he is a watchman relieved of his duty. Like the watchman of Philip Nicolai's hymn "Wake, Awake," he sees that day has come.[13] He can go in peace, trusting that God's salvation is finally here. The word of God, that word which from Genesis promised life to the people, is here. The second verse talks about the eyes of Simeon and of all the people, those eyes which have strained in the darkness to see the morning star. The third verse contains the climactic metaphors, of light and glory. God is revealed in light, Christ's light filling our eyes with salvation just as the day's light fills our hours with life. We have seen Christ's light in baptism, just as we have lived in the light of this past day.

The word "glory" deserves special consideration. The "glory of the LORD" is a central Old Testament metaphor for God. The glory of the LORD settled on Mount Sinai in a cloud (Exodus 24:16), appeared in the tent of meeting (Numbers 14:10), resided in Solomon's temple (1 Kings 8:11), fills the heavens (Psalm 19:1), and shall be revealed in the end time of justice (Isaiah 40:5). Moses, chosen though he is, is mortal and cannot survive the complete view of God's magnificent glory (Exodus 33:18-23). It is as if the noun "glory" gives an image to the reflexive pronoun: God's glory is God's self manifested for us to see and believe. Of course glory is also our praise to God: we are enjoined by the psalms and by Paul to give glory to God by reciting the deeds of the LORD. Glory belongs to God (Revelation 19:1), and we give God glory (Revelation 19:7); both meanings of the word occur together. We go finally, again, to John's Gospel to see this magnificent notion of divine glory turned toward Christ. The prologue states that the glory of God we see is in fact Jesus Christ (John 1:14). Jesus asks to become the glory of God by ascending to his Father on the cross (John 17:5).

Like John, Luke sees the glory of God in Jesus. In his infancy story, God's glory is manifest in the baby Jesus; the helpless infant is the blinding light of God's magnificent being. This baby who calls forth Simeon's praise is the arrived Messiah, the incarnate Word, the light of humanity, the revelation of God's self, the house of God, the very glory of the LORD. Lutherans are accustomed to singing this canticle after receiving communion, as if in

holding the bread they, with Simeon, hold Christ, the
light to all the nations, and are ready with Simeon to rest
in peace.

For Christians the day, the week, and the year re-
volve around the mystery of Christ. The natural
phenomena of light and darkness offer a metaphor for
imaging Christ. In praying the daily office Christians
focus actual time around transcendent mystery. Of
course, when liturgy is exquisite, we have a sense of
being transported into a time beyond time. We traipse off
to monasteries famous for superb liturgy, hoping to
retreat into otherworldly time. But when we talk with
the monks and the nuns, we discover that for them the
services, exotic for visitors, fit naturally into their day
and repetitively, year after year, mark their busy lives
with their baptismal cross. Their discipline of prayer is
more similar than not to the Sunday parish Eucharist for
the devout mother, whose preschoolers during the first
lesson groan that they need a drink of water and during
the eucharistic prayer spill their Cheerios. Christ re-
deems this hour, this day, this year, from captivity to evil,
and in our baptism we are freed for life in this hour as an
hour of salvation.

SECOND THOUGHTS

What this chapter needs is a good deal more realistic
talk about private time versus communal time. At least
for the Western audience that will read this book, time is
increasingly thought of as a private resource, the hour of
each day as a unit of one's personal life in which to slot
one's individual plans. One's choice of how to spend
time determines to great degree the course of one's life:
part of what constitutes a catastrophe is that we did not
plan for it. With options for how to spend time continually multiplying, and with some freedom as to when
tasks actually get accomplished, the business of choosing
what to do when has become a major constituent feature
of many people's days. More and more employers are
offering flex time rather than stipulating vacation days,

in order to enhance the employees' ability to construct their own calendar. In these individualized work schedules, one's religious holidays are accommodated by being construed as personal days. Thanks to VCRs, we can choose even when to watch television programs, thus bending national time to private time. We tend to clutch these decisions close to ourselves, hoping to keep to the self the decisions of how to use the hours of each day.

Liturgical time functions completely differently. The sacred speech describing all three of the units of Christian time — the week, the year, the day — utilizes the imagery of light, and in so doing makes clear that religious time is not about personal decision, but about communal, even cosmic, participation. Our use of electricity allows us more or less to ignore the natural flow of light and dark. Even for a couple lying in bed, one person can be sound asleep and the other reading a book by the beam of a tiny lamp. Understanding liturgical time requires us to imagine back before electric lights, when the availability of natural light determined the activities of the entire human community. As for the week: "Sunday" received its name from the pagan religious sense that the week began under the protection of the greatest heavenly body, the sun. All social activities needed to attend to the natural order of the universe, and so the week's tasks came to be organized not by personal preference, but by the orbits of the planets, of which there were thought to be seven. As for the year: In the northern hemisphere, the year see-sawed back and forth between the summer solstice and the winter solstice, the earth's natural cycle of living and dying providing the central annual festivals for the entire community. Between these two solar poles came significant halfway points, the spring and autumn equinoxes, also times for communal celebration. As for the day: The day too was determined by the rising and setting of the sun, the life of the community reviving each day with the coming of the light.

An enormous contemporary challenge for the Christian community is how to retain this ancient sense of the priority of communal time, without making our religion

96

seeming archaic. The contemporary pattern of many Christians attending Sunday liturgy occasionally rather than weekly suggests lives too busy, people too tired, options too plentiful — perhaps liturgy too boring — but it also indicates how unwilling we are to give precedence to the requirements of communal time. I now stress that our baptized life is life together. We need not live and die alone: our life, for better and for worse, is communal. The community supports and enriches me, and my participation in the lives of others gives my days more meaning, and a quite different meaning, than they could have were they spent all by myself. Our baptism bonds us to God, yes, but also to a community of persons. This bond is one that much in contemporary society cares little or nothing about and will not move an inch to support. Baptized people require participation in the regular communal ritual as a reminder of this bond, in order that we may understand, strengthen and rejoice in it.

My chapter outlines the ways that the imagery of the Christian week, the year, and the day focuses on the light of Christ. Another way to interpret this light is that only in the community of the Spirit of God can we be enlightened by the life of our baptism. At the outset of each week (I use only those calendars arranged so as to begin the week with Sunday) the community rekindles in us the light of our baptism. At the time of the spring equinox, the community reaffirms its faith that God will bring life from death. At the close of each day, we join with Christians around the world in one continuous close of day, the Church constantly committing itself to God, who is the end and the beginning of all.

About Sunday worship, I am as conservative as ever: Christians meet around word and meal on the day of the resurrection. It's fine to meet also on a Wednesday night or a Saturday afternoon, but such services of worship cannot replace Sunday, the day of the sun, the day that God creates the world, Christ rose from death, and the Spirit forms and reforms the community. That the liturgy is lousy is not an excuse for staying home: just go. There you will be reinserted with the community of believers into a time other than your own. Our society no longer keeps Sunday as a partial sabbath, but many Christians throughout the history of the Church have had to fit into the endless tasks of subsistence living their weekly reentry into liturgical time.

About the *Exsultet*: I see that the phrase about "the necessary sin of Adam" has been edited out of the translation of the *Exsultet* provided by the service books of several churches. I agree with many Christians that there has been far too much emphasis in some pieties on personal failures, far too much attention granted in catechesis to the mythic tale of Eden, and far too much nonsense about women ensuing from this androcentric legend. However, I would vote to keep an echo of Genesis 3 in the *Exsultet*, and I hope that it is not only my childhood formation in a conservative branch of Lutheranism that accounts for this opinion. Rather, my observation of human life confirms at least one truth of Genesis 3: what we imagine will better our situation often does not. We choose something for the self and in so doing harm the human community. In trying to enlarge my life, I open the door to death. The Garden of Eden story affirms that there is no human life without death. And it seems to me that in this everlasting scenario, women and men function more similarly than not.

This portrayal of the human as a creature who repeatedly chooses death instead of life is a necessary part of a mature acceptance of Christian life. Such an acknowledgment of the inevitability of failure is one ingredient of our reliance on the Spirit of God in the community for forgiveness, support and guidance. Each year I encounter college freshmen raised in the Church who have not heard the story of Genesis 3 (!!). They are miffed to read that God expels the man and the woman from the garden: isn't God supposed to forgive everyone? It strikes me that the Church too often errs on one side or the other, proclaiming either all human sin or all divine forgiveness. There is not even common sense, least of all the paschal mystery, in such oversimplifications.

About the bees: It is instructive to read Jerome's diatribe against the appearance of the bees in the *Exsultet*. Jerome, the preeminent biblical scholar of the fourth century who produced the Vulgate translation of the Bible, resisted the incorporation of nonbiblical imagery in this great song of the resurrection. "Do you not see the absurdity of it all?" he bellowed, criticizing the entire praise of the candle as inappropriate. Still today debates can rage between the followers of Jerome and the successors of Ambrose, that fourth-century master of metaphor in mystagogical catechesis. The biblical scholars' concern for accuracy and fidelity to the text argues against the liturgists' love of metaphor and elaboration of the image. For healthy Christian liturgy, however, we need both voices, those who call us to stick to the Scriptures and those who show us how religious imagery can fly. But on this one, Jerome, you lose. I wait, late on the Saturday night after the first full moon after each spring equinox, for those bees to buzz their way into our assembly.

Unleash the bees

Sacred Speech about Place

HOLY PLACE

In the ancient world the holy place was revered as
the center of the universe. A particular people or locality
located the center of creation as the primary place of
God's power. The spot might have been a natural phenomenon — a fresh spring, a cavern, a mountain, a
forest clearing, a mammoth tree. A monument, a sacred
pole, or a kiva may have been built to make the locus of
power. At this holy place, this navel of the world, sacred
time was operative, for here at this primordial intersection of human and divine, the time of the gods prevailed.
At this holy place ritual action recreated the world.
When the Israelites enter Canaan, its center is seen as
Mount Gerizim, from which blessings come
(Deuteronomy 27:12). In the Judeo-Christian world, the
holy place is understood as the place of theophany. Here
in a moment of divine revelation God manifested God's
self. The familiar story of Jacob's ladder takes place
where perhaps there already was a holy place for the
Canaanites. The dream of blessing makes the pagan place
sacred space for Jacob: "This is none other than the
house of God, and this the gate of heaven," he exclaims
(Genesis 28:17), and he names the shrine *Bethel*, "house
of God."

The human need for a house of God becomes paramount later in Israel's history. As its culture became
more urban and the people elected a king, they wanted to
have, like their Canaanite neighbors, a temple in the city
for the king. The stories of the desire for a temple, the
building and dedication of the temple, its rituals and
liturgies, its destruction and rebuilding, fill up considerable portions of the Hebrew Scriptures. For Ezekiel the
temple becomes the mythical center of the expected reign

of God on earth (Ezekiel 41). Even though Solomon admits that God cannot be contained in a mere temple (2 Chronicles 6), the building as house of God becomes the locus of religious ritual and the primary symbol of divine presence. Like the awesome burning bush of Moses' vision, the house of God as holy place is a revered place which inspires subjection. The Temple's Holy Place and Most Holy Place are ceremonial areas for only sanctified priests, who alone can approach so close to the divine majesty.

Yet the Old Testament offers an alternate vision. The tabernacle as holy place is not the house of God but the tent of meeting. It was a common tent, rather than a gold-plated edifice; portable rather than erected on a grand foundation; pitched among the people, rather than built for the king; a place of communication with God, rather than a space for reverencing divine majesty. The theological point of the tabernacle was that God resides not in a holy place but rather among the people. The people need not make pilgrimage to a holy place for sanctification; instead, God journeys with the nomads. The development of synagogues during the exile demonstrates this same truth. God is revealed wherever two or three gather to hear God's word, to praise, and to pray.

"Destroy this temple, and in three days I will raise it up" (John 2:19), Jesus says, referring to the temple of his body. For Christians the house of God and the tent of meeting is Jesus Christ, in whom God is manifest and through whom we communicate with God. Christians need not search for the center of the universe, consecrate great temples, or carry about household shrines. Christ is our temple and our tabernacle, our holy place. Paul uses this metaphor in teaching of the Church. Christ is like our temple's cornerstone; the Spirit builds the Church into stones around Christ (Ephesians 2:20). The Church is the dwelling place of God, for where the baptized people assemble around Christ, there is the dwelling of God. In Christ the church is both residence of God and meeting place for the people.[1]

Like other religions, Christianity has its shrines. In the holy land are places made sacred by tradition's belief

that there Christ lived and died. Throughout the world
are places made sacred by stories of the saints and their
interaction with Christ. On this balcony, we say, Francis
of Assisi was inspired to write his Canticle of Brother
Sun; and because there Francis experienced the presence
of Christ, we revere the place as holy. But such holy
places are not essential to the Christian faith. Unlike
Islam, we do not require pilgrimages. Rather we invite
the baptized weekly to the local church, for there is the
place made holy by the weekly assembly around bread
and wine. The eucharist as the presence of Christ hallows the building.

The Church has constructed its holy places on many
designs.[2] The house church functioned as a metaphor for
sacred space because we eat a meal in a home. The great
basilica of San Clemente in Rome is said to have been
built over Clement's house, in which he presided over
worship. The fourth-century basilicas conceived of
sacred space as an imperial judgment hall. The medieval
cathedral with its massive choir set apart the two classes
of Christians from each other. While the cathedral style
may have served the monks well, it was devastating for
the assembling laity. Baroque churches construed the
church as a theater in which gloriously to observe the
action of the performance.

A second early model, tomb of the faithful as sacred
space, saw its own development. The domed eastern
churches — square, round, or cruciform — recall the
practice of assembling at a spot made holy by martyrdom.
Saint Peter's Basilica in Rome is said to be built over the
bones of the apostle. Where a saint has died, there we
assemble to celebrate our death in Christ. Yet other
models exist: the Reformers used the metaphor of the
assembly hall for a meeting place of the people. Contemporary churches have attempted architecture — some
successful, some silly — that understands sacred space as
both the house of God and the house of God's people.
The balance must be struck, for without both dimensions
the building is not uniquely Christian sacred space.[3]
Fortunately, granted all our monstrous mistakes in
church design, Christians can make use of any space for

corporate worship. When the altar and the font are there, a grove of trees, the musty catacombs, a gilded basilica, whitewashed meeting halls, a revival tent, and even the Louise Nevelson chapel in New York City can serve Christians for holy space. The holiness resides in Christ, in the word, in the sacraments, and in the baptized people of God.

The ancient image of the mountain of God provides us a perfect example of Christian sacred space. God's name is revealed to Abram (Genesis 17) as *El Shaddai,* God of the mountain peaks. Historians of religion discover that in many ancient myths the nearest and highest mountain peak is the abode of God. Mount Olympus is only one of many holy mountains that symbolize the dwelling of God. It was on "the mountain of the LORD" that Abraham agreed to offer up Isaac (Genesis 22:14). The Old Testament continues with stories of Mount Sinai and Mount Horeb, on which God is revealed to Moses, the Israelites, and Elijah. At Jerusalem the Temple is built. Although Jerusalem is not actually a mountain, it gains the mythic title of the mountain of God (Isaiah 2:1-3). The transfiguration (Mark 9:2), the betrayal (Mark 14:26), and the ascension (Acts 1:12) take place on mountain tops. In the Book of Revelation, Mount Zion is the mythological holy place, the vision of heaven filled with the baptized clamoring around the divine presence. Yet Christian churches are not built on mountain tops. When the Samaritan woman asks Jesus which is the holiest mountain for worship (John 4:20), Jesus' circuitous answer, echoing the tetragrammaton, concludes, *Ego eimi,* "I am" (v. 26). We leave the mount of transfiguration. It was not very revelatory even to Peter, James, and John. The disciples ran away from Mount Calvary, and they stood confused on the mount of the ascension. Where is our mountain? "I am," says Christ to the woman at the well. Where there is Christ, a well, the word, and a woman gathering her neighbors, there is a Christian holy place.

CHRISTIAN PLACE NAMED

We call both ourselves and our sacred space "church," thus stressing the necessity of the assembled people. Where the church as people gathers, there is a church as sacred space. Our English word "church" derives from a late Greek genitive form of the noun *kyrios,* "lord." A house "of the Lord," *kyriakon,* became a church. With the word "church" we translate the Greek noun *ecclesia,* which in the Septuagint translated the Hebrew noun *qahal,* the assembly. The New Testament uses the word "church" in its various contemporary meanings, the universal body of Christ (Ephesians 5:23), the local congregation (Acts 14:23), and a particular place of worship (Colossians 4:15).

Our word "church" means to evoke the assembly, the people gathered around the word to worship. The whole assembly keeps the Passover (Exodus 12:6); Moses assembled the people before God (Numbers 8:9); Solomon dedicated the temple and blessed the assembly of Israel (2 Chronicles 5:6). The noun implies the action of people coming together; it implies a reason for their gathering. The test for successful church architecture is whether the layout and design of the building facilitate the people's assembling around the word and sacrament as around Christ.

Our word "sanctuary" comes from the Latin *sanctus,* meaning "holy." In some traditions, the word "sanctuary" denotes the entire church building. In others the word specifies the holiest place in the church building, what other people call the chancel. Thus continues the age-old custom of finding protection from one's pursuers by "taking sanctuary" in a sanctuary. The first definition is the happier for Christian exegesis, for clergy do not require or create a holier place than that of the laity. The word "chancel," from the Latin word *cancellus,* meaning "balustrade," originally meant the railing that divided the clergy from the laity. Many contemporary churches are designed to eliminate such a medieval hierarchy distinguishing clergy and laity.

A term with happier connotations is the word "nave." From the Latin word *navis,* meaning "ship,"

comes this metaphor of the church interior as a boat.
Like the ark, our ship rides the waves of the primordial
waters of baptism. The metaphor, rooted in 1 Peter 3:20-
21, is used explicitly of the church building as early as
the year 375: "When you call an assembly of the church
as one who is commander of a great ship, . . . let the
building be long, with its head to the east, so it will be   *East*
like a ship," reads the Apostolic Constitutions.[4] As with
all metaphor, we ought not take the image literally and
design our churches in the shape of a ship. Instead, we
enrich our pews with the metaphor, sitting on the
benches of our nave and sailing home to God.

St Peters - West

CHRISTIAN PLACE IMPLIED: THE *KYRIE*

Some of our liturgical texts and actions imply a
sacred space which is left unnamed. These implied
metaphors are significant for our full appreciation of
Christian liturgy. For example, the presidential prayer of
the assembly is modeled on court address. The succinct
linguistic style, the naming and praising of the monarch,
and the clearly stated request reflect the format of petition to the Roman emperor. Thus, our prayer form
implies that, like Esther petitioning the king, we come
boldly to the imperial court seeking aid (Esther 5:2).
This metaphor is embodied by the basilica of Saint Mary
Major in Rome, the interior a massive gilded throne room
of the church's queen.

In sharp contrast, the reading of the lessons implies
a small synagogue in which the faithful share the word of
God. One from their midst — a local student of the
Torah, surely not a monarch — rises to read the lessons.
Among those readers in centuries past was Jesus himself,
donning his tallith and proclaiming the lesson from
Isaiah (Luke 4:16). Later in the liturgy we prepare the
table for a meal. Bread and wine are brought forward, the
vessels made ready. The throne room turned synagogue
is now turned dining room, home of the Emmaus disciples (Luke 24:30) sharing a meal with the risen one.

Yet another sacred space, the *Via Dolorosa*, is implied in the *Kyrie*. This responsive petitionary prayer,

"Lord, have mercy," has been sung at the beginning of the liturgy since the fourth century. When the Latin rite adopted the practice, the Greek litany was retained. The phrase echoes the pleas for mercy in the psalms: and while Psalm 51 is a famous psalm of penitence, more commonly (as in Psalm 123:3), "Have mercy upon us, O LORD" is a plea for deliverance and for social justice. In the synoptics the phrase is used by the leper and the blind for healing. *"Eleison me, Kyrie,"* calls out the Canannite woman (Matthew 15:22). Paul uses the word "mercy" to mean God's forgiving kindness (Romans 11:30). Yet it is not likely that these biblical references gave rise to the liturgical petition. *Kyrie eleison* had a long history in the Greek world as a phrase used to welcome the sun and later to laud the emperor. We might imagine a pagan facing the sun at daybreak or townspeople hailing the monarch who processed through the countryside. Like the exclamation "God save the Queen!" *Kyrie eleison* was a shout of praise and at first took the form of a litany offering prayers for the whole world. Not until medieval times did it acquire the heavily penitential quality that so many of its musical settings suggest. *NOT PENIT.*

The word "mercy" means God's compassion, the compassion humanity needs if it is to survive in the face of evil and before the face of God. We do not stand up well before either death or divinity. And so we cry for mercy. We ask God to be more gracious than magnificent, more forgiving than righteous. We plead for release from the pains of our humanity.

When we cry, "LORD, have mercy," we take the prayer of the prehistoric sun worshiper, the Hebrew psalm writer, the Greek emperor worshiper, and the maimed first-century Canaanite woman and offer that prayer to our God, the LORD, who is Christ, our Lord. Our sun is our emperor, is Jesus walking on the road, is our God. The prayer turns our room into the *Via Dolorosa*, the way Jesus walked, the roads of human life trod by God. Our prayer is strong, not simpering. It offers us imagery from the entire history of religions and culminates at the hill of Golgotha. We must not interpret this prayer as a stale statement of God as male monarch. The term "LORD," as we have seen, offers us great heights of metaphoric meaning, provided that we have not fallen into the pit along the way. The way we Christians praise the parading Lord is to stand by as Jesus walks on to the cross.

CHRISTIAN PLACE TRANSFORMED: THE *SANCTUS*

Another text we sing each Sunday, filled with mingled metaphor, is the *Sanctus*, the "Holy, Holy, Holy Lord" sung during the great thanksgiving prayer. In this chant several sacred spaces are implied: in fact, if there is any spot in the liturgy when we are transformed out of our nave and into a transcendent place, it is during this chant, for the power of its images is meant to transform our common space into the holy place of God.

The *Sanctus* has been part of our praise since the Jewish synagogue worship. We sing it as part of the eucharistic prayer, for the preface calls us to join with all the angels of heaven to praise God. Appropriately, our song is a quotation from the seraphim who surround God's throne with fiery praise. While in the Jerusalem temple, Isaiah sees a vision of God's transcendent holiness, and the angels are singing "Holy, Holy, Holy is the LORD of Hosts" (Isaiah 6:3). Again in the apocalypse the creatures around the heavenly throne join the angels in chanting, "Holy, Holy, Holy is the Lord God Almighty" (Revelation 4:8). Both visions attest God's majesty. In Isaiah, all space, heaven and earth, is filled with God; in Revelation, all time — past, present, and future — is filled with the Lord. The Hebrew word *sabaoth* seems to refer to the maintenance of Israel's heavenly armies. The contemporary translation renders this obscure word "power and might," not so much to be antimilitaristic as to avoid confusion with the word "Sabbath." So in these first lines of the hymn we are caught up with Isaiah and with John in ecstasy in the Temple, on the Lord's Day, into heaven, into a vision of God's transcendent power and might.

We then switch holy places. From the heavenly temple we go to the dusty streets of Jerusalem where not fiery angels but faithful Jews line the path, not to the throne but to the cross. On the first day of Holy Week, Jesus comes riding into town on a donkey, the monarch's symbol of peace, and in their expectation for the coming of the messianic age, the people of Jerusalem chant the ancient words, "Hosanna! Save, we pray!" Singing the Passover Hillel psalm (Psalm 118), the people acclaim this Jesus of Nazareth as "the One who comes," using a messianic title to praise Jesus as the LORD's anointed. In the ancient world the term "the name of the LORD" functioned as a circumlocution for the LORD's very self. In our pews we join with the people of Jerusalem to laud Jesus on a donkey as the one who comes with the power and might of God.

John's Gospel adds other images by referring to the palm branches the people waved (John 12:13). Palm branches recall the Jewish feast of Tabernacles. This feast, like our Thanksgiving Day, occurred in autumn as a celebration of the harvest and inspired a week-long pilgrimage to the altar in Jerusalem. The feast recalled God's dwelling with the people in the desert and celebrated God's presence in the Temple. For the feast of Tabernacles, Psalm 118 proclaimed the joy of those who enter the house of the LORD. John's interpretive technique leads us to say that the one who enters the Temple is Christ.

Thus when we sing these five simple lines, we call to mind many metaphors: Isaiah's vision in the Temple, John's vision of the heavenly throne, the singing fire of the seraphim, the road to Jerusalem, the path to the cross, the Passover cry of "Hosanna," the messianic hope for "the One who comes," the Tabernacles' joy at thanksgiving, the praise of the Temple, and God's presence with us in our desert and at our altar. God in the Temple, on the throne, on the donkey, in the desert: this God we praise with all the angels as we attend the bread and wine. We see before us bread and wine, but in our liturgy we see God in the fire of the throne, God in the cloud in the desert, Christ in the dust of the streets. With these metaphors we affirm our faith in the presence of God in our midst, on our altar, and in our bread and wine, with a vividness that philosophical definitions about the real presence can never approach. "Holy, Holy, Holy" is our best metaphoric statement about Christian sacred space. Here in this church we sing, "Holy, Holy, Holy" — holy to God who is holy, holy in this place which is holy by its word of Christ and its sacraments of the Spirit. We need not literally journey to Bethlehem or Jerusalem, for at this sacred space around this bread and wine we have our vision of God. "Show us the Father," pleaded Philip (John 14:8), and Jesus gathered the disciples to himself.

SECOND THOUGHTS

The metaphors Christians use to describe their sacred space are not merely randomly or creatively chosen imaginative pictures that alter our perception of our meeting room. Some of these metaphors recall the history of Christian worship. We call that piece of furniture a table because in the first century it was indeed literally a dining room table. Within a religious tradition, sacred spaced develops over the centuries, with the past remaining alive through the current metaphor.

We are provided with a typical development of sacred space in the long history of the southwest Native American kiva. Archeologists have demonstrated that anciently the peoples we now call Pueblo lived in pit dwellings, below the surface of the ground. Around a thousand years ago they moved their communal residences to be above ground. However, in a religious nostalgia so common among humans, they retained the pit dwellings as sacred spaces, set apart as the site of holy ceremonies. And, demonstrating an androcentrism pervasive around the world, only men were allowed into the kivas. Still today, activist Native American women claim not to know or care what goes on inside the kiva. An example of the difficulty we have in facing ancient religious symbolism is the wall painting in the kiva at the

Kuaua Pueblo in New Mexico. The reconstruction of the paintings that depicted the necessity of rain has obscured the original image in which rain is portrayed as sperm spraying out from the body of the deity.

We can trace the pattern: (1) Anciently, people reside and dine and dress and bathe in a certain way. (2) In time, the living patterns change, and the ancient way is retained as sacred and becomes stylized into religious ritual. (3) Oftentimes, the sacred way is reserved for the males. (4) This history gives both pride and embarrassment to later religionists.

This pattern can be applied to much of also Christian sacred space. Let us think, for example, of the church building as a gathering place for hearing the word. Anciently, the tribe would gather around a fire to hear their family stories. The book of Genesis suggests that many of these stories were about the favored wife and successful childbirth. As the society grew more complex, it was no longer feasible to gather around the fire to listen to great-grandmother tell her tales. So storytelling became formalized, stories became codified, and the meetings set at certain times of the sun's journey. By the time of the Deuteronomic tradition, the privileged storytellers were men, with women denied any participation. Of course the women continued to tell stories around the fire, but this commonplace activity was not deemed holy.

Centuries of development brought us to the synagogue, a local building in which the men met weekly for their sacred storytelling. Such a synagogue provided the locus for Jesus to read and interpret the prophet Isaiah (Luke 4:14-21). Christians inherit this campfire-turned-synagogue and continue it to the present. We are rightly proud of maintaining the archetypal human desire to hear the stories of the past, and we deal variously with the historical pattern that only men could tell and interpret the stories in the holiest place. As well, we take the religious situation as a model for daily life: we encourage one another to tell stories at home, to honor our own family history, to read from the Bible daily at a family

110

meal, to remember the lives of the saints. That is, in
various ways we live out the values of the pit dwelling
although we now live above ground.

The pattern applies also the way that Christian
sacred space has evolved from the dining room. I read in
the real estate section of the newspaper the horrendous
advice that you ought not purchase a house with a dining
room. If you do, you will later discover you can't readily
sell the house, since nobody uses a dining room any
more. Well, I say that Christians do, or ought to, in
dining room or kitchen or somewhere, continue the
ancient human tradition of meeting one another around
food and of finding in that encounter not only a more
satisfying meal but also the mercy of God. We need to
find ways to counter the contemporary practice of "graz-
ing" and to enhance the mealtimes of the many
Christians who live alone. (I asked my daughter how
folks who don't read the Bible after dinner know when
the meal is over. She said, "They turn off the TV.")

As well, any parish activity which interferes with
family meal times ought to be rescheduled. It would be
counterproductive to teach the metaphor of meals, to tell
all the biblical stories of meals, to instruct everyone
about the Passover, to make our eucharistic practice
better recall communal meals, to replace wafers with
pita, but then to set committee meetings during dinner
time. Meals, of course, are not merely eating. A meal is
eating made deeper, longer, an occasion for feeding both
body and spirit by speaking with one another and by
together thanking God. Perhaps when people join your
parish, they could be presented with a candlestick and
candles in the liturgical colors for home use. Metaphors
are not only thought about in the head, but also enacted
in daily life.

What remains a quandary for all of us engaged in
religion is to what degree religion is, like recalling the pit
dwelling, merely the romance of the archaic. The path-
way of the emperor that stands behind the *Kyrie*, the
throne room that determined Western Christian prayer
rhetoric, the temple setting of the *Sanctus*, the *Via*

Dolorosa recalled in the *Benedictus*: this is all ancient history. I for one demand a religion that is quite up-to-date. All its evocation of the past must serve to enliven the present and to guide the future. The liturgy cannot deteriorate into nostalgia for a past world that never was as flawless as we like to imagine. The metaphors in Christian liturgy must not function like Grade B movies that mindlessly fill up a stray hour here and there with images of happy pioneers who had great fun on their pleasant walk across the beauteous prairie.

Concerning the cosmic mountain: It is fascinating how often in Western speech what is "up" is better than what is "down." As the *Sanctus* suggests, God is "in the highest." The stock market goes up, we say, and back-packers delight in climbing mountains in order to experience a "high." Unfortunately, this symbolic patterning many times over the centuries got extended to include males, who were up, and females, who were down. Reversing the medieval practice in which the chancel, the holiest place of the church building, was elevated from the floor of the nave and reserved for males, some contemporary church architecture situates the altar area central to the space, lower than the seating, and of course welcoming to women. Recalling not a cosmic mountain, but rather a sacred pool or divine womb, the floor plan suggests that we are all gravitating toward the central space as into God. The cruciform design of a medieval cathedral can give way to a more circular space, shaping the community of the Spirit around the water, the word and the meal.

In my chapter I suggest some of the holy spaces that are metaphorically resonant within the classic texts of the liturgy. I now add to that list the metaphors behind our regular praying of psalms. The psalms have a polymorphous ancestry. Some seem to have been the poetic compositions of individuals in joy and praise, sorrow or lament. Others are sacred chants borrowed from neighboring religions and only minimally altered to refer to the Israelite deity. Some exalt the life of the scholar, others narrate the history of the people, others glorify a male monarchy. Thus at the origin of the psalms are various spaces — a house, a temple, a school, a pilgrimage route. Yet, as each psalm was canonized into the hymn tradition of the Israelites, it took on wider meaning. The space was no longer the individual home, a local temple or the royal court, but was the community center in which the people of God gathered around the promise of the covenant. Later on came the Levites, the male-only chorus. But now, among both Jews and Christians the psalms fill our sacred spaces, synagogues and churches that metaphorically superimpose the ancient sacred sites into the present location in the hope that the blessing of God available back then is available also to us.

One last word concerning the *Kyrie* and *Sanctus*: As is characteristic of the classic liturgy, a primary word in these texts is "Lord." The *Kyrie* alternates "Lord" with "Christ," and the *Sanctus* names "the God of power and might" as "Lord." Thus all the issues raised in Chapter 4 on Lord/Lord apply also to these beloved and problematic texts.

Wrestle with The Kyrios

— 8 —
Sacred Speech about Objects

Holy Things

The biblical idea of holiness begins with the understanding that "holy" is the primary description of God. God is holy, and thus awesome, majestic, terrifying, wonderful. God is other, separate from humankind (Isaiah 6:1-5). When people or places or objects are ritually set apart as signs of theophany and vehicles of blessing, they too are said to be holy. The priests' task (Leviticus 10:10) is to distinguish the holy from the common. The later development of the Holiness Code (Leviticus 17-26) is also related to worship: only those with cultic purity are worthy to be set apart for God's service. That which is holy to the Lord is set apart as an offering to God and becomes a vehicle of grace.

This word signifying divine distinctiveness is translated into the Anglo-Saxon *hal,* meaning "whole." That which we call holy is whole, a sign of God's creation, unbroken, filled with meaning. By means of religion, human beings seek to restore their own wholeness and attempt to make time and space newly whole. Religions focus on certain objects — elements of the universe and crafted things — as signs of wholeness in God's redeemed world. Already in the beginning of the second century Hippolytus' church order indicates blessing formulae not only for bread and wine but also for oil, cheese, olives, milk with honey, and water for drinking.[1] But when the Orthodox priest calls out, "Holy things for the holy," the choir responds, "One is holy, One is the Lord Jesus Christ." If Christ alone is holy, what do Christians mean by calling objects holy?

Anthropologists talk about *mana*, using the Melanesian word meaning infused holiness.[2] *Mana* is the terrifying yet attractive power of death turned into a

114

force for life. Granted by the spirits of the dead, *mana* changes living people and natural and crafted objects into extraordinary religious entities from which emanate salvific power for the whole community. Something of this idea of *mana* is behind the synoptic story of the hemorrhaging woman who is healed by touching the hem of Jesus' garment. In the long account in Mark 5, Jesus perceives "that power had gone forth from him," and he searches for the one who touched him. Mark 6:56 again recalls this *mana*-like quality of Jesus' garment, for many who touched even his clothes became whole.

But Matthew treats this story differently. He edits out all of Jesus' acknowledgment of the holiness of his garments. The woman tries to touch his hem, but Jesus intervenes and, commending her faith, heals her. Furthermore, Matthew places this pericope directly after Jesus' teaching (Matthew 9:14-17) about the new garments. He warns that we are not to put new patches on old garments, but to get ourselves new garments altogether, new wineskins. It is perhaps not coincidental that these two narratives about garments are juxtaposed. Perhaps Matthew, who retains in 14:36 the memory of the holiness of Jesus' garments, wants, like the liturgy of John Chrysostom, to say that "one only is holy." We believe in Christ, not in holy things. Christ is not merely a new patch on the worn Judaism of the past: Christ is a whole new garment — a baptismal robe, if you will.

Thus the tension about holy things occurs already in the Scriptures, and it continues until the present. Some contemporary Christian pieties are uneasy about ascribing holiness to things. They do not ritually bless things and do not practice patterns of reverence towards liturgical objects. Other pieties are overloaded with blessings for every object associated with worship, from the altar to the paschal fire, and they maintain folk traditions in which farm animals and pets, homes and fishing fleets are blessed, signed by the cross, made holy to some degree, and given life from God. Perhaps because there has been such diversity in this matter — and the differences do not lie conveniently along denominational lines

— the West has not been clear in articulating its idea about holy objects. The East has its icons and a well-developed hermeneutic of the icon as the sign of the incarnation, the created thing through which we travel, in the mystery of Christ, towards the vision of God. But in the West we have folk blessings for some, canonical rituals for others, and, for summer evenings, the Grail legend, that Arthurian tale of the sanctity of the cup used at the last supper and the blessings which that chalice bestowed on Sir Galahad, who alone was pure enough to attain it.[3]

Because there is no ecumenical consensus on holy things, we have little choice of common texts for our analysis. Those traditions which do bless objects use a variety of verbs: "set apart," "bless," "dedicate," "consecrate." These verbs themselves have different connotations. Furthermore, very little has been done to bring classic notions about holy things in line with contemporary phenomenology. We do not hold any longer to Aristotelian physics in which reality can be divided into substance and accidents. Contemporary theories of perception instead postulate that there is only one reality of which we can speak, that this reality is the only reality we know, and that we know this through human perception. Thus our perception constitutes our knowledge of reality. Our calling an object holy means something different from what it meant to a natural scientist of the thirteenth century.

Let us begin with the fundamental word "bless." Blessing is a divine action. It is done by God to the chosen. The salvation history of Israel is a tradition about those God blessed, why, and how. God gives life, God saves the people, God blesses Abraham, Isaac, and Jacob. In the Aaronic blessing the presider asks God to bless others: "May the Lord bless and keep you." Ritually important figures, like priests, and cultural authorities, like patriarchs, have the right to lay that blessing on others. So Isaac blesses Jacob (Genesis 27:28-29). Their social position suggests that their plea for God's blessing will have effective power.

In the psalms we continually bless God. That is, we acclaim the life of God. We sing out that our God is the one who is life and who gives life. Our praise to God, our blessing God, is our affirming that God is the one who has the power of life; God is the one who owns the right of blessing. In "The LORD will bless us . . . . May you be blessed by the LORD . . . . But we will bless the LORD from this time forth and for evermore" (Psalm 115:12, 15, 18), the word "bless" occurs in its various usages. The Hebrew word *berak* describes the reciprocal relationship of the covenant: God gives us life, and we give God praise; God blesses us, and we bless God.

In religious ritual we bless God not only with our voices and our songs but also with natural and crafted objects. For example, we bless God with the organ. That is, the organ joins us in praise; it assists our praise; it is set apart for praise; it symbolizes our praise. So in Psalm 103 and in Francis's Canticle of Brother Sun, the whole created order praises God; with the holy universe, the universe made whole in God, we join in blessing.

Furthermore, we say of these objects with which we have blessed God that they themselves are blessed. "Whatever you, O Lord, have blessed is blessed for ever" (1 Chronicles 17:27). By this we mean not that objects have a magical power in themselves, but that these objects join us in blessing God. As Hippolytus wrote in his list of blessings, "But in every blessing shall be said: 'To you be glory, to the Father and the Son with the Holy Spirit, in the holy Church, both now and always and to all the ages of ages.'"[4] To bless bread and wine, oil and cheese meant to set apart these objects in order to bless God in the church. Because God is holy, there can be holy things for the holy.

The figure of Melchizedek gives us an image with which to apply the word "bless." Melchizedek, the king of Salem and priest of God Most High (not God YHWH), blesses God YHWH for salvation, acclaims that Abram has been blessed by God, and ritually offers bread and wine (Genesis 14:18-20). The writer of Hebrews uses Melchizedek as a metaphor for Christ. Christ comes as priest and king, blessing God, blessing us by God, and offering himself (Hebrews 7:26-28). The blessing from God comes to us through the mediation of the one holy king and priest, Christ. Christ bears the blessing of God, and so we are blessed, as we join with Christ to bless God, offering Christ himself in bread and wine. In the mosaics in Ravenna and throughout Christian iconography, Melchizedek is a metaphor not only for Christ but also for the priest at the Eucharist who in offering to Abram and to us bread and wine seals the covenant of blessing with God. The bread and wine are made holy by signing for us wholeness with God, God's blessing of us and our blessing of God.

We could say that there is *mana* in Christian liturgical objects, if by that *mana* we mean the Spirit of Christ. At creation God's Spirit hovers like a nesting bird over the whole universe. God's Spirit is bestowed uniquely on us creatures formed carefully from dust, but the Spirit of God fills the whole world as well. Our setting aside some natural and crafted objects as signs of our praise acknowledges that God's Spirit hovers over our worship as the Spirit of the risen Christ.

BREAD AND WINE

For nearly all Christians the most revered objects in worship are the bread and wine. That reverence may be great or small, but it is more reverence than is awarded anything else in the liturgy. Theologians are always trying to explain what happens to the bread and wine to render these common foodstuffs our holiest objects. The apostolic fathers began by commenting on the scriptural passages. Gregory the Great popularized a literalist interpretation, in which the physical change of bread to body accounted for our attendant reverence. The scholastics, and particularly Thomas Aquinas, using Aristotelian categories of substance and accidents, described the spiritual change that occurred. The Reformers with their nominalist philosophy had to choose between Luther's mystical claim that the bread was both bread and body, and Zwingli's symbolic interpretation that the bread symbolized the body. The faithful have martyred one another over these philosophical and scientific explanations of the primary liturgical language. The liturgical language — that bread is body — cries out for our most intellectually respectable hermeneutic.

Ecumenical reconciliation on this point need not be for anyone a denial of historical statements. We need not take back what Aquinas or Trent or Luther or Zwingli said, any more than we have to choose between Paul's "proclaiming the death of the Lord" (1 Corinthians 11:26) and John's "eating the flesh of the Son of man" (John 6:53). Instead we must search together for contemporary philosophical language that articulates the mystery of our sacred bread. Edward Schillebeeckx offers a possibility in his use of contemporary phenomenology.[5] Which contemporary language will describe the real presence of Christ in the Eucharist without calling forth the ridicule of philosophers and physicists? Schillebeeckx begins by pointing out that for us personal encounter is constitutive of reality. We do not think as though there were an external reality, independent of whether we observe it well or poorly. Instead, we think of human perception and interpersonal encounter as constituting the only reality of which we can speak. Christ is really present in the Eucharist. That is, in these created forms God gives the assembly the person of Christ, and our communal reception of Christ among us constitutes the Eucharist. The bread and wine are signs of the *Parousia* already, a beginning here and now of our being the body of Christ in the resurrection.

While we rejoice at the possibility of ecumenical consensus, theological explanations like transsignification are not part of liturgical language. In the liturgy we deal with biblical images formed into ancient prayers. Here our attention is caught by two texts: the great prayer of thanksgiving, which puts words around our blessing of the bread and wine, and the words spoken during the distribution.

The eucharistic prayer, commonly called the Great Thanksgiving, is most likely derived from the *Birkat-ha-Mazon,* the Jewish meal prayer. Like that Jewish prayer, the Christian Great Thanksgiving praises God for being God, for creating the world, and for saving the people. Christians praise especially for the person of Christ, crucified and alive again and present uniquely in this very meal. The prayer includes an *epiclesis,* an invocation of the Holy Spirit, and after praying petitions for the coming of God's reign, concludes with a doxology.

Characteristically the prayer's blessing culminates in praise for the life of Christ. The biography of Jesus includes the relative clause "who on the night in which he was betrayed," which leads to a liturgical narration (not a direct biblical quotation) of the words of Jesus over bread and wine at the last supper. Remembering these words and the salvation given us in Christ, we offer the bread and cup with our praise. This *anamnesis* and offertory is variously worded in the many eucharistic prayers now current, but the sense is usually that in remembrance of Christ we praise God, we pray this prayer, we offer ourselves, and we offer bread and wine in our praise. As in the Common Eucharistic Prayer, "we now celebrate this memorial . . . . Recalling Christ's death . . . and offering to you this bread and this cup, we praise you and bless you."

The old designation of this prayer as the Consecration Prayer suggested that the words of the prayer effected the consecration of the elements. Thus interminable arguments arose over the idea of a moment of consecration at which the specific words of the presider functioned like magic to change bread into Christ or to add the body to the bread. The move to suppress the designation of consecratory prayer indicates contemporary consensus that such a notion misinterprets liturgical language and misunderstands Christian praise. The prayer is not a magical formula. The prayer is praise of God for the person of Christ. Like Melchizedek of old and the host at Jewish meals, Christians offer their praise with bread and wine. The bread and wine — symbols of God's creation and human industry, both our sustenance and our joy — join us in our praise. We say they too are blessed, made holy by providing for our liturgy the mode for the presence of Christ among us.

As we receive the bread and the cup, words repeat the promise that Christ is made known in this breaking of bread. Roman Catholics say simply, "The body of Christ, the blood of Christ." United Methodists and Lutherans add, "given for you." Episcopalians include the metaphors "the bread of heaven" and "the cup of salvation," adding Hebrew images of manna and seder cup to the Greek terminology of body and blood. Here is liturgical language at its purest. We have not even full sentences, only phrases that, when spoken as the people commune, name the bread and wine to be the body and blood of Christ. There is no explanation. There are not even verbs. We have only the words of faith, language used strangely .The bread does not look like body, the wine does not taste of blood. This is not literal language. It is supreme metaphor, not as image contrary to fact but as religion, reality re-created by the power of the resurrection. The bread is not "changed" to body; the bread does not "represent" the body. Both verbs are too weak to articulate our faith. In this act, in our praise of God with our offering of bread, the body of Christ is manifest among us. Let the people say Amen!

After "Holy, Holy, Holy" we sing, "Blessed is he who comes." Blessed be God. Blessed be he who comes. Blessed are we who bless him who comes. Blessed is the bread which he is among us. Bread is a holy thing for the holy people because it is our primary locus of the presence of Christ. One only is holy, one is the Lord Jesus Christ. As the bread is for us the body of the Lord, it is our holiest thing.

The Altar

By extension from the bread and wine we revere the altar. We require something to keep the bread and wine off the floor; that we call this piece of furniture an altar is a masterpiece of metaphor.

The Hebrew word for "altar," *mizbeah,* comes from the verb meaning to slaughter, just as our word "altar" comes from the Latin verb meaning "to burn up." The etymology of our sacred name for a simple table indicates

the first stage of its meaning: the Old Testament refers to
the practice of ancient tribal sacrifice in which by burning up life to God, God's force for death is appeased
(1 Samuel 7:9). There is considerable debate concerning
what the Hebrews, and later the Jews, imagined their
sacrifices to be effecting, and it is difficult to sort out the
primitive literal understanding from a later theological
development towards metaphor.[6] While the burning of
incense to typify our praise indicates the metaphor of the
altar, the four horns of the altar, most likely primitive
phallic symbols, suggest ancient ideas of the altar as the
repository of divine power. While the psalm sings joy-
fully about processions around the welcoming altar
(Psalm 118:27), some of the narratives are much more
literalistic: Abraham ties down first his son, then a ram,
to slay for God (Genesis 22); Elijah follows the
Canaanite ritual in offering a bull to the LORD (1 Kings
18). To the extent that either the uncut stone or the
gilded box served as a symbol of God's presence, the
sacrifice of animals or the burning of incense indicated
Israel's communication with God. The altar is both a
sign of God's fire forever burning and the place of our
covenanted response. These images of the altar occur
also in the Book of Revelation. The altar is guardian of
the perpetual fire of God (Revelation 8:5) and the place
for our offering incense and prayers (8:3). The martyrs
under the altar plead for justice (6:9-10). The altar itself
praises God (16:7).

But Abel, Noah, Abraham, Moses, Joshua, Gideon,
David, Solomon, Elijah, and all their sacrifices notwithstanding, Christians do not have an altar. We do not
dedicate phallic stones. We do not slay animals to God.
We do not contain God in a box. We go up the mountain
not like Abraham to slay a ram but like Moses and the
elders to eat and drink with God (Exodus 24:11). Eating
with unclean folk was one of Jesus' primary offenses
(Mark 2:16), and when the Gospel writers record the
disciples' experience of the resurrection, we have stories
of meals: supper at Emmaus (Luke 24:29-30), fish on
Sunday night (Luke 24:42-43), breakfast by the sea (John
21:13). In contemporary church design the altars look

again more like tables: scaled to recall a table, positioned
to center our common meal, covered with a linen that
resembles a tablecloth more than a brocade pall or the
upholstery of a throne.

So we have religious metaphor. We construct a table
and treat it as if it were a table. Its function is to hold up
the vessels for our meal. Perhaps as for a formal dinner
party, we grace the table or area with candles. The host
presides, serving the bread and wine as if offering a feast
for our plates. Yet we name this table an altar, for our
meal is the death of Christ. Our food is his body, which is
this little bit of bread. The upper room gains its significance from Golgotha. In our rituals of dedication,
although we laud the altar as the place for the meal, our
actions and our vocabulary recall sacrifices of old. Some
traditions prefer to call the altar a table, and currently
the hyphenated "altar-table" is used.[7] Yet our instincts
for religious metaphor urge us to call our table an altar.
If the table is merely a common table around which we
feast, it is not the table of the Lord. If as an altar it
becomes a holy box for the presence of God, guarding
relics of the LORD, it is not the altar outside the city wall
of which Hebrews 13:12 speaks. The Christian altar is a
table, and the table of the Lord the only altar we need.

WATER FOR BAPTISM

A blessing of the water is not required for valid
baptism. For emergency baptism we recognize that
ordinary water is God's creation, a sign of new life and
the symbol of our regeneration. The water does not need
to be made especially holy. Yet for many Christian traditions the full ritual of Baptism includes a blessing of the
water. By this we mean that in a prayer of thanksgiving
we bless God for the water and with the water, and we
ask the Spirit to use this created element as a sign of
divine blessing upon us. From this arose the use of holy
water, the blessed water recalling past baptisms and
signing again our cross-inscribed forehead. The prayer
for the blessing of God over the baptismal water is remarkably similar in the Roman, Episcopal, and Lutheran

rites.[8] The Roman prayer is longer, for it explains each biblical image with theological interpretation. But the flow of images is the same in each prayer and constitutes our sacred speech about baptismal water.

All three prayers begin by praising God for the "gift of water." Here we acknowledge that creation is God's gift to humankind, ours not by right or chance but by divine providence. Already this ordinary tap water (perhaps we have gathered at a flowing stream, but probably not) is God's gift, a sign of God's continuing salvation for us all. The prayers then recall the primeval waters of creation over which the Spirit hovered. For the ancient Hebrews, land is stable but the sea is chaotic, the waters being a sign of the inexplicable power of death. This explains the promise that in paradise the sea will be no more (Revelation 21:1). But the Judeo-Christian story of creation gives God power over the primeval deathly depths. The Spirit tames the waters and turns them into the gift of water for us all. Thus the prayer has set up the paradoxical metaphors: water as gift of life, water as chaos of death. Both metaphors are stretched, for it is the common water before the blessing which we call gift, and it is the raging waters of primeval chaos over which the Holy Spirit moves.

The prayer of thanksgiving now blesses God for the history of water rescues. Two of the prayers praise God for saving Noah in the flood. The New Testament uses that story as metaphor for baptism (1 Peter 3:20-21), the flood waters, like baptismal water, carrying us through death on to life and to the worship of God by the dove under the rainbow (Genesis 9). The prayers liken the water to the sea through which Moses led the people of the Hebrews, out from the death of slavery to the freedom of the promised land (Exodus 14). Our baptismal waters, like that sea, show red with blood, not from the veins of our enemies but rather from the dying Jesus. In the sixteenth-century painting by Jean Bellegambe, at the base of the cross there is a baptismal pool filled with the baptized frolicking not in clear water but in the blood flowing down from Jesus' wounds. Each prayer then likens the baptismal water to the Jordan River, the water

124

in which Jesus himself was baptized and anointed with the Spirit (Mark 1:9). It is interesting that in ancient baptisteries the depiction of Jesus' baptism often shows the old man of the sea, the monster of the deep, being submerged as Jesus rises from the water.

The prayers, then, sum up the Christian meaning of these metaphors of water at creation, the exodus, and Jesus' baptism, by evoking Jesus' death and resurrection. The cross is the primal chaos, the slaughter of the Egyptians, and the destruction of the sea monster. The resurrection is the hovering Holy Spirit, the song on the safe side of the sea, and the alighting of the dove. With these metaphors we call water blessed, sanctified by its participation in the death and resurrection of Christ. The prayer now invokes the Holy Spirit upon the water. Recalling the Spirit over the waters of creation, the olive branch over the flood, the pillar of fire across the sea, and the dove at Jesus' baptism, we pray that this water too can give new life to all the baptized. Our going down into the water of the font is our descent into the death of Christ. Our rising from the waters, like emergence from the womb waters, signals our coming to life in the Spirit. The water seals our forehead with the cross, the water washes us into new life, the water flows with the Spirit. We do not change the common noun. We still call it water, but the water now has sacred meaning for the assembly.

THE FONT

In calling our vessels for baptismal water a font, we recall the Latin word *fons,* meaning "spring of water." Before Christians crafted fonts, they used the water from flowing streams. When fonts were moved indoors, many were round, recalling the womb of the second birth. Others were cruciform to recall the cross, and still others were sunken pools suggesting descent into death. By the time infant baptism became normative, the river had become a tub or bowl on a stand, sometimes designed to suggest a chalice. Ornate carvings of beasties suggested the forms of evil that were drowned in the baptismal waters.[9] Yet few of our fonts have been what the word implies, a spring of flowing water, water alive with the life of the Spirit (John 4:14).

The biblical images to support the font as a spring of water come from the apocalyptic writings. At the end time, on the great day of the LORD, water will flow from Jerusalem to all the world (Zechariah 14:8); water will spring up from within the temple to fill the land with life (Ezekiel 47:1). On the feast of Tabernacles, the remembrance of Solomon's temple and the time of prayer for autumn rains, Jesus applies the call of Isaiah 40 to himself: those who are thirsty should come to him and drink (John 7:37). Out of the heart of Jesus flow rivers of living water. The water flows not from Solomon's temple but from Christ the temple; not from the city Jerusalem but from Christ the abode of God. To be baptized is to be brought into membership in the city, to stand in this temple of God. To be baptized is to be overwhelmed by the flowing waters of Christ. Let us retire the finger bowls and the silver shells of the past liturgical practice to a museum of ecclesiastical oddities and return to the use of substantial fonts of flowing water, the better to signify the waters flowing forth from Christ.

SECOND THOUGHTS

The Church in our increasingly informal society needs to give careful attention to holy things. Clergy presiding in jeans leaning against the altar, the hard crust of the loaf of bread crumbling all over the floor, baptisms conducted in plastic kiddie pools: such incidents reflect a society that worships the casual. Assemblies will come to different decisions about what objects they term holy, which objects they revere as signs of divine wholeness. Yet churchwide diversity on these issues ought not suggest that nothing can signify the holy or be in a concentrated way a conveyor of God's mercy.

Concerning the words spoken at the distribution of the bread and wine: Although no church's service book prints out this new wording as standard or even optional, there is a growing practice in various denominations that the person serving the bread or the cup addresses the communicant by name. Calling out "The body of Christ, Jane," is yet another example of our informal social patterns, suggesting that a worthy presider knows, recalls and is authorized to use everyone's first name. Such a practice fits well with American individualism, for it pinpoints the mercy of God directly to me.

But before we regularize this inculturation, we need to think critically about what is lost, as well as what is gained, in this significant alteration of sacred speech. I argue that one thing that is lost — besides respect for presiders who blank on names — is the communal meaning of "the body of Christ." It is the bread shared in the community that is the body of Christ, the gathered assembly together that comes to embody the body of Christ. The intimacy of the divine exchange that is suggested by the use of one's first name gives ritual centrality to a privatized medieval spirituality which much twentieth-century liturgical theology has sought to correct. As members of the body of Christ, we all receive, consume and become the body of Christ. I am not convinced that hearing my first name murmured by someone who softly touches my palm will enhance my communal understanding of the baptized life. I am more intrigued by the possibility of presiders calling out loudly, before each person, "The body of Christ for you all."

Concerning the blessing of the water: Blessing prayers nearly identical to the ones in Roman Catholic, Episcopalian and Lutheran worship books are now included also in United Methodist, Presbyterian, United Church of Christ, and other Protestant churches' service orders. This phenomenon is what has been termed "the ecumenical liturgical consensus." The similarity in texts is the work of a generation of liturgists who sought common liturgical language in our ecumenically-shared history and in ecumenically-determined translations. A recent interest in texts that are specific to one's denominational, ethnic, socio-economic or sexual situation brings with it the advantage of liturgical inculturation, but the danger of yet more Christian fragmentation into small self-groups. We need continued wisdom as to which texts are to be shared in common and which can express more narrow communities of prayer.

My chapter considers those "holy things" necessary for the celebration of both Eucharist and Baptism, their elements and their furniture. Were I now writing a chapter on holy things, I would include the proclamation of the word by elucidating "Bible" and "lectern."

Our word "Bible" is not a translation of any word, but rather a transliteration of the Greek plural word for "books," *biblia*. Although Greek-speaking Christians referred to our Old Testament as Scriptures, the term Bible became the standard designation for all the books, both the Old and New Testament together. Recently, concern that Christians honor the Jewish history of three-fourths of their holy book has led to suggestions of other terminology, at least in biblical studies: the "Hebrew Scriptures" or "First Testament" are heard as replacements of the classic terminology "Old Testament." A far more controversial discussion is also underway: were the books chosen for our Bible the right ones? What about attention to those gospels and epistles that were rejected in the canonical decisions made in the second century?

Yet such debates notwithstanding, it is the word "Bible" that has a central place in Christian sacred speech, and, as with the words used at the distribution of communion, it is unfortunate that the plural nature of the term has been lost. Of course the Bible is a single book that the Church reveres. Yet it is also a library, many books, written by many people over many centuries, their remarkably varied voices narrating, praising, lamenting, exhorting, chronicling, prescribing, the many styles and tones themselves a metaphor for the diversity within the Church. Yet Christians call this motley book holy, for we revere it as a sign of divine mercy and a conveyer of grace. Like all metaphor, the Bible is holy only in an ambiguous way, and our lectionary systems give evidence of the Church's on-going debates about where in the Bible we can most readily encounter that holiness.

The popular practice of parishes printing out the Sunday readings has had at least two unfortunate results. Inaudible or sloppy reading has been tolerated, since people are able to follow along with their printed text. In many churches, the lectors are not trained to be sentries on the tower, calling out the arrival of God. Secondly, minimal ritual attention is being given to the thing that is the book itself, to the Bible that is proclaimed, since many lectors read from a little piece of paper they have in hand.

I believe that holy things matter, that ritually honored objects enhance our liturgy with their symbolic resonances. Thus I advocate that, when the lector needs the reading to be printed out, for example in order to alter the translation toward inclusive language, the translation be set inside a magnificently bound and designed Bible. The Bible should be carried in procession and held before the assembly as if it mattered. After all, it is the focus of our attention for the first half of our celebration. I would like the pages of the Bible to be so stunning, perhaps with illustrations, that after locating the passage, the reader will pause for a moment of awe, silenced by the beauty of the pages. I would like all the people to rise for the reading of the Gospel and to sing the "Alleluia," in respect for the word that is Christ now speaking within the assembly. If you dislike my ritual suggestions, I hope you find other ways to demonstrate that in this Bible we encounter the holy word of God.

Concerning the lectern: Contemporary church design is moving away from providing two pieces of furniture, one a relatively plain reading desk and one a symbolically elaborate preaching podium. Many churches now have only a single lectern. The noun "lectern" derives from the Latin word "to read." Whether or not we think of this piece of furniture as a holy object, we ought to construct it to be worthy of its task: to bear, perhaps even to enthrone, the holy book from which we read.

I have not included in this chapter discussion of an object that many Christians deem holy: a cross. The cross came to be revered by Christians in the fourth century.

Before that, it was a repugnant reminder that the lowest members of the population were executed in a totally inhumane manner and, for Christians, a sign of the scandal of the incarnation. However, when Emperor Constantine outlawed crucifixions and his mother Queen Helena, on her archeological search of Jerusalem, discovered what she claimed was the True Cross, the cross became a revered sign of both power and piety. Those contemporary Christians who consider the cross a holy object had best attend to a single worthy cross in their midst and retire the dozens of crosses here and there, embroidered on ushers' lapels or functioning as the stopper of the wine cruet. Thoughtless multiplication of an image is more likely to trivialize than to enhance it.

What is most ecumenically acceptable is not that any specific depiction of a cross be honored, but that the signing of the cross be maintained. Martin Luther wrote that upon waking in the morning, "you are to make the sign of the holy cross and say, 'Under the care of God, the Father, the Son, the Holy Spirit'." The cross signed on one's body repeats the gesture made upon us at baptism. It places the cross not on a wall but onto the self. When I sign myself with a cross, I place myself under the cross, asking the triune God to bless me through the cross. Perhaps in this instance the action is more fully expressive than the object.

— 9 —
Sacred Speech about the Assembly

It might surprise a twentieth-century person how little talk there is in the liturgy about humankind. Thomas Merton once wrote, "In an age where there is much talk about 'being yourself,' I reserve to myself the right to forget about being myself, since in any case there is very little chance of my being anybody else."[1] Something of this comic paradox is characteristic of liturgy, that while we remain very much ourselves, we are freed from talking about it all the time. The psychological movement, in calling us to be self-aware, has marked "contemporary" liturgies with continual references to the self: "We are here in the name of Jesus Christ. We are here because we are men . . ." began the popular liturgy of St. Mark's in the Bowery.[2] Some contemporary prayers are riddled with references to the self: "We have grown weary pursuing justice, despaired of peace that is so hard and slow . . . ours is in emptiness made of haste."[3] Feminist liturgies are characterized by their continual references to the feminine self.[4] But such talk is not the content of the historic catholic liturgy.

There are several reasons why the liturgy contains little talk about the self. The ancients were not publicly verbal about, perhaps not even interiorly aware of, their self-reflective consciousness. It was, after all, only Erik Erikson who popularized the term "identity crisis."[5] Furthermore, the language of identity is individualistic. Who am I? we ask. Psychoanalysis tends to isolate the person in diagnosis and in cure. But the liturgy is a communal expression of corporate faith. The medieval focus on individual penance and Protestant preaching on personal salvation are far from the Bible's corporate metaphors of the life of faith: the children of Abraham, the people of Israel, the disciples, the body of Christ. To the extent that psychological categories separate us into individual case histories, they are inappropriate metaphors of the self for liturgical use.

The liturgy provides us with its own metaphors for our identity. There are metaphors of us as sinners, in the confession of sin; often the lessons speak to the sad condition of humanity; burial rites reflect images of what it means to be mortal. There are positive images of humanity as well. The absolution recalls our baptism. Our standing boldly to pray implies a redeemed humanity, a renewed self-identity as part of a people before God. We shall examine the pronouncement of Ash Wednesday and the invocation of the Holy Spirit at baptism for their metaphors of Christian identity.

DEATH AND ASHES

One of the strongest metaphors the liturgy employs to describe the dark truth of human existence is in the line "Remember that you are dust, and to dust you shall return." These words are said on Ash Wednesday as the presider traces an ashen cross on the foreheads of the faithful. With this ritual Lent begins. Our word "Lent," both appropriately and paradoxically comes from the word meaning "springtime." (What a fine metaphor!) Lent is the forty-day preparation for Easter. The season was originally the time to prepare catechumens for baptism. Later it became a time for disciplining public penitents. By the eleventh century the disciplining of public sinners had evolved into a penitential rite with the imposition of ashes for all the baptized. Ashes, that which remains after sacrifice, were a sign of humanity before God. Appropriately, ashes were used in rituals of penitence. The ashes of the liturgy are the residue of the burned palm branches left over from the previous Holy Week. It is as if the greens with which we praise God — and hasten the crucifixion — become the ashes of our own self-identity.

Especially when most Christians are baptized as infants, Ash Wednesday is an important ritual of identity. The day and its metaphors allow the faithful to

132

rehearse each year the dynamics of their baptism. For adult catechumens there is first the awareness of their humanity, second the time of purgation, and finally their entry into the Christian community. The same dynamics are present for the believer observing the paschal cycle. Ash Wednesday grants a deepening awareness of one's humanity, Lent focuses on baptismal growth in grace, and finally, the Easter Vigil celebrates the baptismal covenant. There is no need to talk about granting baptism only to adults. God's grace comes to the infant as well as to the adult, and the liturgy gives the baptized adult the time from Ash Wednesday to Easter each year to renew more deeply the mystery of the event.

The words "Remember that you are dust, and to dust you shall return" contain two basic truths about our condition. In the first place, dust is a metaphor for our mortality. In the creation story, God creates human beings out of the dust of the earth, enlivening that dust with divine spirit (Genesis 2:7). After the fall, Adam and Eve can no longer share God's immortality or enjoy the fruits of the tree of life. Human mortality — returning to dust — is a result of the knowledge both gained and lost in the fall (Genesis 3:19, 22). The metaphor of dust can be traced in the Hebrew Scriptures (Psalm 104:29, Ecclesiastes 12:7): although life comes from God, after death the human body returns to dust. Abraham uses this metaphor as he pleads for the residents of Sodom and Gomorrah, "Behold, I have taken upon myself to speak to the LORD, I who am but dust and ashes" (Genesis 18:27). It is his very mortality that Abraham confesses before the immortal God. Finally also Job "repents in dust and ashes" (Job 42:6) for his effrontery in challenging God. Recall that Job is innocent: he is not confessing sin, but pleading his mortality before the God who created the universe.

The second referent for the metaphor of dust is human sin. The Israelites sat in ashes as a ritual of penitence. At the Easter Vigil we hear of the king of Nineveh, who, heeding the call of Jonah, symbolizes his repentance with ashes (Jonah 3:6). In Daniel 9:3-19 the king sits in ashes to symbolize the penitence of all his people. As part of the Ash Wednesday liturgy we pray Psalm 51, which legend says was David's lament of repentance after committing adultery and murder. "Wash me from stain, cleanse me from guilt." It is perhaps relevant that in the ancient world ashes were used as soap, a vehicle for cleansing.

In the metaphor of dust we say two things of our-selves. We are mortals who cannot stand before God and live. One day we too will be dust; as the classic burial committal has it, "We commit this body to the ground, earth to earth, ashes to ashes, dust to dust." Even in the too lighthearted new Roman rite for Ash Wednesday, a prayer pleads, "Lord, bless these ashes by which we show that we are dust." Second, in the metaphor of dust we say of ourselves that we are sinners who cannot bear God's righteousness. Lent calls us to turn our lives around, so that we enact God's grace. Both metaphoric meanings of dust, mortality and penitence, should be evoked. Christians want neither fascination with death nor obsession with guilt. That we will die, that we sin — this is the human identity. Whether pleading our mortal-ity like Abraham or confessing our sin with David, we are dust.

ALIVE IN THE SPIRIT THROUGH BAPTISM

Dust is metaphor for only half of our identity, for we are *baptized* dust. The Spirit of God has been breathed into us. We begin Lent in dust, but we conclude at the font of the Easter Vigil with the metaphors of our second identity. These metaphors are found in the invocation of the Holy Spirit spoken after baptism, at the laying on of hands, or at confirmation.[6] The prayer, addressed to God as the Father of our Lord Jesus Christ, describes the baptized person as freed from sin and risen to new life and prays for an outpouring of the Spirit who will grant the gifts of the Spirit. Each of its phrases answers to the condition of our dust and ashes.

The prayer begins by addressing God as the father of our Lord Jesus Christ. Far from retreating meekly into our mound of dust, we stand boldly invoking God. This

God was called *Abba* by Jesus, and since we are baptized into the body of that Christ, we are members of God's family and children of that loving father. We shall not be rival gods, as the serpent suggested; we shall instead be children of a loving God and part of the household of Christ.

We baptized people are freed from the power of sin. The metaphor is of sin's ownership of its slave. Evil can dominate our decisions as in Eden and can physically command our actions, as the New Testament exorcisms attest. In that we are as dust and guilty, but we have been forgiven. We as baptized people arise to new life. The image is of a newborn baby, arising from the baptismal waters to live anew. God bears us again in the pains of divine labor and we are reborn, covered with the blood and water flowing from the side of Jesus. In that as dust we will die, we have been given new life.

Recalling the creation story, the prayer invokes God's Spirit on this dust. The list of the gifts of the Spirit comes from an oracle of the coming messianic king (Isaiah 11:2). The one who sprouts from Jesse's stem will display the spirit of wisdom, understanding, counsel, might, knowledge, and the fear of the LORD. We pray that in our baptism God's Spirit will give us the same qualities Jesus had. That is, for Christians, the Spirit of God is the Spirit of Jesus. By God's Spirit we too are heirs of the kingdom, along with Christ, the messianic king. We bear in ourselves the body of this Jesus, now at God's right hand.

This invocation includes all the primary metaphors of our life as baptized people of God: we are children of Jesus' father, freed from slavery to sin, born to new life; we are heirs of God's reign and members of Christ's body. Other metaphors are contained in the rituals that follow baptism. The anointing marks us with the *tau* of the end time, the cross of Christ (Ezekiel 9:4, Revelation 7:31); the white robe signifies our being washed clean from sin's stain (Hebrews 10:22); the lighted candle likens our new life to illumination by the light of Christ (John 9:7). Dust, we are, but freed — dust reborn. Martin Luther used the phrase *simul justus et peccator,* "simultaneously saint and sinner." As Paul said, "Dying, and behold we live" (2 Corinthians 6:9).

WITH THE NEEDY: THE INTERCESSORY PRAYER

It is not enough, however, for Christians to know what the assembly is in itself. The identity of the Church is always determined by its identification with all the suffering of the world. Francis of Assisi both prostrated himself before the cross and embraced the leper. In spite of the glorious metaphors for Christian identity in the baptismal invocation of the Spirit, we are empty if we do not embrace the lepers and take their suffering into ourselves. The primary place in the liturgy where we enrich our Christian identity by identification with the needy is in the intercessory prayer. In the second century Justin wrote that after the homily "we all stand up together and offer prayers."[8] This prayer of the faithful took on the form of a litany. Sometimes its format is of bids. An example is in Good Friday's bidding prayer.

The intercessory prayer pleads for blessing on all the world. We pray for the Church, the world, nations and leaders of nations, local government, the community, all who suffer, all who are needy, all who are ill. We pray that God will remember the dead and fulfill the divine promise to bring the faithful to life again. The first and last petitions are for the Church, living and dead. But in the rest of the prayer we offer before God the whole needy world, even our nation's enemies, our non-Christian neighbors, all the sick and needy and dying. It is as if the faithful are doing all the praying for the whole world. Before God we also are needy, in trouble and near death. The lot of the needy is our lot. We are the leper.

The intercessory prayer is pitifully misunderstood when it functions as a rehash of the sermon, a bulletin board for parish activities, or a catalogue of our pet projects. Nor is this prayer the time for consciousness raising. We plead with God to act; we do not only ask that our attitudes be altered so that perhaps *we* will act. The prayer lifts before God all the world, not just ourselves. Most intercessory prayers are too short — there is much that needs our prayer. Yet even a prayer that is too short can be laborious if it is read poorly or if in convoluted prose we tell God and the congregation how to solve the problems of the world. Perhaps the best format involves extremely simple petitions ("For the poor, . . .") followed by short silence. Such open bids form the people into one prayer, allowing for the interior shaping of specific requests by each one present.

WITH THE SAINTS:
THE VIRGIN MARY AND MARY MAGDALENE

There is yet a final metaphoric expression of who we are as Christian assembly. We identify not only with the needy but also with the saints. This may occur on All Saints' Day, on days of memorial for parish and denominational leaders, or with the full sacral calendar of saints' days and commemorations. Many eucharistic prayers state that we offer our thanks in the company of the saints; in the United Methodist prayers, the *Sanctus* is sung with angels and saints. Perhaps in naming our congregation Saint John's we mean to petition John's prayers in our behalf; but also we mean to identify with John, hoping to become beloved disciples. The saints are the baptized who though dead are alive again in the body of Christ. Their godly example inspires us; their failings prod us; their baptism links them with us to Christ. We call also ourselves saints, the living who in baptism have died and are alive in the body of Christ.

The saint *par excellence* is the virgin Mary. Even Christians who avoid talk of saints preach about Mary's obedience. We cannot consider the stories of Jesus without recalling Mary's role at Jesus' conception and birth, rearing, first miracle, death, and resurrection. The Church's theologians found that thinking of her as God-bearer *(Theotokos)* provides a key to our understanding of Christ. Much has been written about Mary in the Scriptures, in theology, in piety, and in symbol.[9] But our concern here is liturgical metaphor. The virgin Mary is an image of grace.

Like us, Mary is made of dust. She is the humble maid of Nazareth whom God calls to bear God's Word. Luther writes that she "seeks no glory, but goes about her usual household duties, milking the cows, cooking the meals, washing pots and kettles."[10] She claims nothing for herself, and this is not in order to vaunt her own humility. Rather, she obediently hears and accepts God's word. In her faithful obedience she becomes a vessel of God's love. She praises God's goodness (Luke 1:46), meditates on the incarnation (Luke 2:19), cares for the Word in her midst (Luke 2:48), prays for those in need (John 2:3), watches at the crucifixion (John 19:25), and receives the Spirit on Pentecost (Acts 1:14). Mary's story is an example of human discipleship. Recalling her faithfulness, the church sings her *Magnificat* each night at evening prayer. Tradition has it that she died on August 15, so on August 15 we celebrate her death, identifying with her in her death.

Mary is also full of God's Spirit. We call her blessed and holy, for she is filled with grace. The traditions of her assumption and coronation suggest that she has already come to the fullness of God's reign, the first of God's creatures to attend the throne of God. Like her, we can be filled with grace. We too some day will rise to dwell with God.

Mary is the maid of Nazareth and the queen of heaven. She is both the humble girl and the mother of God. She is the image of the Church and a Jewish woman. The ancient councils expressed this paradox of grace in their christological title of "virgin mother of God." Can a virgin be a mother? Can God have a mother? Christian truth grows within the cracks of human language.

Other descriptions of Mary point to this paradox. Mary is the new Eve, both like and unlike Eve. She is the daughter of Zion, the bride of Christ, the mother of the Church, all at once. Mary is the dwelling of God — pregnant woman, the ark of God, and the image of the Church. Grace visited Mary with the divine without removing her from the human situation, and that miracle is the Christian mystery.

The ecumenical Church must find ways to venerate Mary as both maid and queen. If she is only a maid, the implications of her connection to Christ have not been considered. If she is solely a queen, the depths of the incarnation have not been fathomed. Hers is both the white veil and the jeweled crown, and ours as well. Our talk of Mary, our interpretation of her as receiver and participant in grace, is a prelude to talk of ourselves as graced ones. Mary is maid and queen, and we are sinners and saints. As we allow Mary to contain the paradox of grace, so we probe that paradox for ourselves. It is easier to play the role of sinner or to glory in our sanctity than it is to live within the paradox of being both sinners and saints, people alive because we have died, people who will live again after we die again.

With a life radically different from that of the virgin Mary, Mary Magdalene affords us a similar metaphor of our identification. It is said that on July 22, 886, the bones of Mary Magdalene were entombed at Constantinople, and on July 22 the church remembers this complex figure. From her Jesus cast out seven devils (Luke 8:1-2). She stood by the cross (Mark 15:40) and was the first person to see Christ after the resurrection (John 20:11-18). For this she is revered as an apostle, sent by Christ to proclaim the resurrection This Mary is one whose previous life was evil and chaotic, and yet who is honored as central to the post-resurrection community. Neither the virgin Mary, graced as she was throughout her life, nor the disciples were the first to witness the risen Lord, but it was this woman, who had once been possessed by devils. That ought to give us all hope!

In its imaginative way the Church sought to tell more of Mary Magdalene's life. Since the time of Gregory the Great she has been identified both with the penitent woman who washed Jesus' feet with the precious ointment (Luke 7:38) and with Martha's sister who sat at Jesus' feet listening to his words (Luke 10:39). Historically, of course, it is unlikely that all these Marys were one. Mary, the Greek form of the Hebrew name Miriam, was a popular first-century name, in honor of the Hebrew leader. But the linking of these stories explains the nature of Mary Magdalene's depiction in Christian art. Usually she appears as a penitent prostitute, with long golden hair unfastened and curling to her waist, and wearing bright red clothing. To the Dominican order, with its call to biblical study, she is the symbol of contemplation, reading the word at the feet of Jesus. The images of prostitute and contemplative are metaphoric expansions of the images of Mary Magdalene as exorcised sinner and as witness to the resurrection.

The virgin Mary and Mary Magdalene appear together in much Christian art depicting the crucifixion. The Virgin is usually standing in sorrow, heavily swathed in dark blue, a veil covering her hair, perhaps a wimple her neck. Mary Magdalene is shown clutching the foot of the cross in frenzied contemplation, her red dress and her red hair signs of her fallen past. At San Marco in Florence, Fra Angelico painted the lamentation after the crucifixion, the virgin Mary holding Jesus' head and Mary Magdalene holding his feet. One Mary is full of grace, yet the other Mary, in a different way, is full of the same grace. The two most revered women in the history of the Church, one lauded as virgin mother, the other infamous as a repentant whore, stand together at the foot of the cross. We join them there, some of us baptized as infants, some known for the life of faithful and humble service, others converted as adults after a wild life and much-needed forgiveness. It is not, of course, as virgin and whore that the Marys are models for us. It is as bearer of Christ and as witness to the resurrection that they are models for all Christians, women and men. In the twelfth-century Church of the Holy Marys in Taizé, France, the women are not mourning and penitent. The Virgin appears in a majestic Theotokos icon, honored with a candle, and Mary Magdalene offers her open hand to the Lord in a stained-glass window that, positioned over the church door, signifies the life of discipleship. Metaphorically, both Marys are us all.

SECOND THOUGHTS

I have much in this chapter to amend and to correct.

Just a comment concerning Ash Wednesday: Ash Wednesday is the annual event that most clearly refutes the claims of the megachurch movement that contemporary Americans will tolerate only up-beat language, simplistic metaphor and no ritual. Ash Wednesday is an astonishingly popular observance in the life of the Church. More and more parishes in a lengthening list of denominations are adopting the ritual of the imposition of ashes. It seems that at least once a year people want to hear and to express the truth: yes, I will die, yes, I am a sinner.

Concerning baptismal metaphors: One reason to conduct parish baptisms in substantial communal celebrations is to rehearse for ourselves all those central metaphors of our identity that are part of the text and ritual action of baptism. A renewed observance of Lent does the same. Were our baptisms and Lents alive with baptismal metaphors, there would perhaps be fewer adults who, not remembering the event of their childhood baptism, ask to be rebaptized. The baptismal event goes on perpetually, renewed continuously by the metaphors of each baptism and of every Lent.

Concerning the intercessions: I am often rendered heartsick by the inadequacy of the Sunday intercessory prayer. The freedom that most churches exercise, to prepare their own intercessions each week, needs far more training and discipline before it can serve as a profound expression of our identification with all who suffer. Too many intercessory prayers are homiletical, written either by the preacher, who understandably sneaks in a petition or two confirming the topic of the sermon, or a parishioner more or less delivering a lay homily. Far too many intercessions are what I call selfish prayers: count the number of times the words "we" and "us" recur. Most prayers are too short, as if four petitions are all that the people, or the clock, can bear.

For here is the truth that is indeed difficult to bear, week in and week out: that placed before us is an endless list of people who suffer, and that as the bearers of the Spirit of Christ in the world, it is our obligation to attend to them. And this means not only our relatives who are sick, or the soldiers on our nation's side of an armed conflict. As the call to prayer in the *Lutheran Book of Worship* has it, we pray for "the whole people of God in Christ Jesus and all people according to their needs."

The intercessions should be objective, nondirective and comprehensive. By objective I mean that the petitions ought not express the emotion of the person crafting the prayers. In order to be graciously open to the entire praying community, prayers should be written with an objective, rather than a subjective, tone. By nondirective I mean that the petitions are to be offered in great humility. The bids should avoid instructing God, or the congregation, how the world's problems are to be solved. Prepositional phrases beginning with "for" are usually better than clauses beginning with "that." By comprehensive I mean thoroughgoing, encompassing many concerns. The text of the intercessions cannot be completed until Sunday morning after one reads the newspaper, since today's news is one of the sources for our prayer.

The classic form of the intercessions followed a medieval Great Chain of Being that began up on top with the Church, traveled down through the world stage and finally got to the sick in our community. Perhaps a different order could be tried — although an expected order of some kind is helpful for focusing the minds of the assembly. It is good, furthermore, if the person leading the prayers is praying, rather than reading bids: the difference has to do with tone of voice.

Now, concerning the saints:

Although centuries of Christian piety juxtaposed Mary with Mary Magdalene, heightening the contrast between the two women by talking about a queen and a whore, I now refuse to participate in perpetuating this tradition. In revering biblical saints, I keep to their minimal biographies as recorded in Scripture and to the first-century memories of their deaths. I do not honor the elaborate medieval legends that got stuck on to them. The more I have read, the more I have come to realize that both Marys were "like Eve" especially in this, that the legends about them were invented by males who were probably quite unconscious of the sexual undergirding of the religious constructs they formulated. Luke praised Mary's obedience because of his views on church order; the medieval church made of Mary a gracious welcoming Queen because it had made of God an inaccessible wrathful Judge; the doctrines of the immaculate conception and the assumption reflect, more than anything about Mary, the desire of a male church hierarchy to assert its own authority. The Gospel of Mark speaks better of Mary Magdalene than it does of Mary. Indeed, the process by which male theologians turned Mary Magdalene, the woman whom the early Church called "the apostle to the apostles," into a ravished prostitute exemplifies the dangers of our viewing the opposite sex as an alien "other" and, as such, a threat to wholeness in the self.

Some Christian women view veneration of Mary to be a helpful balance in a male-dominated Church. Indeed, C. G. Jung advocated that the Church elevate Mary into God, turning the Trinity into a quadrinity and in this way including the feminine in the divine. However, since I do not understand God as male, I do not need Mary for a counterweight. To teach about Mary now, I explicate the *Magnificat*, that psalm-like praise of the God who turns the established order upside-down. In the canticle of Mary, which monastic communities teach us to pray each evening, the servant does not become a queen — all the better for her, since the mighty are going to be cast from their thrones. The *Magnificat*, in asking God to remember the promise of mercy made to our ancestors, pleads for all the lowly and hungry of the world. We honor Mary because God lived within her, just as God lives within all the lowly of the world. Either extreme — ignoring Mary or making her into a semigoddess — misapprehends the mercy of God as revealed in the Judeo-Christian tradition.

In teaching about Mary Magdalene now, I like to contrast the biblical passages that explicitly mention Mary Magdalene with those later attached to her, as a way to examine our continual human habits of negative stereotyping and sexual accusation. The gospel for July 22, Mary Magdalene's Day, is the resurrection story from John 20. The first reading recalls Ruth of old. Like Ruth, Mary Magdalene thinks that she is surrounded by death. Yet, thanks to the mercy of God, she encounters new life, and she rushes off to proclaim the resurrection to those who are still cowering in their rooms. Forget the off-the-shoulder outfit.

To teach about our identification with the saints now, I urge people to attend with creative delight to the sacral calendar. I do not mean merely the calendar approved by one's church, although that is one place to begin. I mean a far more diverse and ecumenical calendar of the men and the women whose colorful truths silence our pale legends. Here's a partial list, traveling chronologically through the centuries, to add to Mary on August 15 and Mary Magdalene on July 22: Peter and Paul, on June 29; Perpetua, March 7; Ambrose, December 7; Augustine, August 28; Radegund, August 13; Hildegard of Bingen, September 17; Francis of Assisi, October 4; Thomas Aquinas, January 28; Catherine of Siena, April 29; Julian of Norwich, May 8; Martin Luther, February 18 (his last words: "We are beggars, this is true"); Elizabeth of Leeuwarden, March 27; John Bunyan, August 31; for American Lutherans, Henry Melchoir Muhlenberg, October 7; for American women, Lucretia Mott, November 11; Oscar Romero, March 24; Dorothy Day, November 29.

If you don't like this list, make up your own; if your list includes more men than women, you've got more work to do. For biblical persons, I stick to the Bible. If I want fascinating biographies, I read history. Our identity as Christians is shaped both by the poor and by the saints. Each week in the comprehensive intercessions we encounter those who suffer, and through our honoring the many saints we come into oneness with a polyglot crew of outstanding countercultural characters. We are to identify with these saints, not only with our favorites on the list, but in some way with each one of these extraordinary baptized persons. A thorough sacral calendar provides a welcome diversity of persons for us to honor, a treasure chest full of gems to try on.

— 10 —
Learning Sacred Speech

THE CHILD: *ABBA*, AMEN

We have seen that even a single word in the liturgy can call forth pages of commentary. Indeed, there is no end to our discovery of Christ in liturgical language. How do we teach all this to others? How can the riches of liturgical language be available to all the faithful? In a society that is increasingly biblically illiterate and symbolically stunted our task is twofold: to tell the stories of faith so vividly that the countless allusions are familiar and to sharpen the skills of the faithful in symbolic interpretation. These two objectives — concerning the images and their appropriation — shape the basic catechetical instruction for each baptized person, which will be repeated in greater detail over and over again through life.

We cannot expect the ancients to offer us theories about the religious education of toddlers. Not until the Enlightenment did adults speculate much about what was appropriate in the rearing of small children. But much nonsense has been written recently about the catechesis of small children. Much contemporary discussion of catechesis is influenced by the developmental theories of Jean Piaget. Many now suggest that certain biblical images and ideas must not be taught before a certain age.[1] While it is true that humans travel through rather predictable stages of cognitive development, rearing a child in the faith is not mainly a matter of cognitive maturation. Thus, stages of cognitive development, even if reasonably accurate, cannot dictate a child's liturgical participation. The baptized child grows up in the life of the Church, participating emotionally, through symbols, years before the child's cognitive responses are like those of adults. To be baptized is to

146

worship God, to assemble weekly, and slowly, slowly, to grow deeper into that baptized life of grace. This liturgical life is open to the toddler no less than to the adult. Bringing the child to the liturgy is more like holding the infant up to grasp the Christmas tree needles than it is like sending an adolescent off to private school. Liturgy is the embrace of God through the assembly.[2] It is not instruction about God through graded materials.

Children grow up into the language of faith in the same way they learn ordinary speech. During infancy they hear countless sounds they do not yet understand; prenatal studies show that the fetus already can hear music. Little by little the child learns the definitions of words, their vast connotations, their emotional content, the acceptable grammar, and finally, we hope, creative linguistic use. This learning progresses first by a kind of unconscious osmosis, then by family encouragement, and later by classroom instruction. So it is with the baptized child. By attending the liturgy from baptism on, the child learns little by little the congregational responses, the ritual actions, and the biblical stories, the liturgy providing the foundation on which family support and formal instruction build. Many mothers tell of overhearing their preschoolers singing the liturgy to their dolls. Children are in fact superb liturgists, emotionally open to symbol and intellectually free with interpretation to an extent often lost by Western adults.

It is a happy accident that *Abba* is such a key word in the Christian kerygma. For many children the babbling of *abba* is the first formation of syllable. We know *Abba* as the divine name that Jesus used in prayer to God. *Abba,* in Aramaic, is the child's nickname for the loving father, a word close to our "Papa", "Daddy." Paul, writing Greek to Greek Christians, quotes the Aramaic word before he renders it with the formal word "father" (Romans 8:15, Galatians 4:6). It is likely that Luke's version of the Lord's Prayer, which begins simply "Father" (Luke 11:2), is closer than Matthew's version (Matthew 6:9) to the actual prayer practice of Jesus.[3] *"Abba,"* Jesus prays in the agony of Gethsemane (Mark 14:36), the cry of the child trusting in the loving parent.

So the child's first prayer, said from birth on, with hands held together or outstretched, is "Abba, Amen." I am the helpless child at the mercy of a loving God — yes, that is my self-definition before God. In four easy syllables the child learns the name of God given at baptism, *Abba*, and repeats the assembly's affirmation of Christ — Amen. It is the whole language of faith for the eight-month-old infant, and it is a worthy core vocabulary on which to build. The infant's babble has been turned into prayer, the cry of Jesus, and the shout of the assembly.

At baptism the parents and godparents promise that they will teach the child the Lord's Prayer. So the child progresses from *Abba* to the Our Father, and the Lord's Prayer said in the security of the crib at night under the parent's smile becomes linked with the Lord's Prayer prayed before communion in the liturgy. Whether or not contemporary Christians revive the use of the Aramaic *abba,* the emotional content of the Lord's Prayer as the trusting prayer of the beloved child can be formed during the child's first two years of life.

At baptism the parents promise to bring the child up in the practice of the faith. The family brings the child to church, and at the Eucharist the very young child begins to say the responses of the faithful, first with the "amen." *Amen is* the Hebrew word meaning "surely" or "truly," and the assembly uses the cry repeatedly to unite itself with liturgical speech around liturgical action. Eventually we teach the child that our *amen* is our YES to Christ, for we speak this Hebrew word in the tradition of all those who saw in Jesus their YES to God and God's YES to them (2 Corinthians 1:20). Neither *abba* nor "amen" is a natural religious term. To name God as loving parent caring for the beloved child and to come together acclaiming the life of prayer: these are postures of faith. This is the liturgical life in two words: "Abba, Amen!" Even the infant can begin to participate.

THE ADULT: THE NICENE CREED

For perhaps 500 years Christians spoke no creed during the eucharistic liturgy. The first-person singular statement of faith was affirmed at baptism. That practice is the origin of our Apostles' Creed. But at the Eucharist it was enough to say amen to the eucharistic prayer, which in its praise of God the creator, its remembrance of the death and resurrection of Christ, and its invocation of the Spirit, functioned as confession of the faith. To be Christian was to pray in a certain way. But the christological and trinitarian controversies of the fourth and fifth centuries required from the Church a specific creedal statement that over the next few centuries found its way into the liturgy as the people's response to the homily. Today most service books suggest the communal recitation of the Nicene Creed as appropriate for festivals and optional for ordinary days.

The child learns "Abba, Amen," and later the Lord's Prayer, but the child will also mature in the language of the Church. Children are to receive a lively education in the biblical stories. Adults have a second layer to explore. The root metaphors of our liturgical language are biblical, and those images come alive in scriptural narratives. Yet the Church has developed its statements of faith in subsequent centuries, applying contemporaneous philosophical categories to develop coherent creedal formulas. Our liturgy is not simply strings of biblical metaphors. These metaphors are structured into doctrines the adult Christian is called to address, creeds fought through and hammered out by orthodox theologians for whom affirmation of certain verbal formulations was a life-and-death matter. We stand in the tradition of Athanasius, the Cappadocian fathers, Augustine, Luther — saints who were philosophical defenders of the faith, intellects whose genius arranged the biblical metaphors into theological statements. Our recitation of the Nicene Creed affirms our place in this history, acknowledging that the Church's theology is an essential ingredient in the meaning of liturgical language.

The Nicene Creed speaks in the plural. It was a corporate statement of conciliar faith: We the Church believe this. This "we," which had become "I" for the medieval priest worshiping alone, has been restored in the contemporary translation. The creed is not a private confession of faith to be mumbled head down, but a corporate profession of faith to be acclaimed for all the world to hear. The "we" reminds us that though we are many, we are one in Christ, united in our baptism.

A draft of the Nicene Creed appeared at the Council of Nicea in 325. Its intent was to combat the beliefs of Arius, whose language about the subordination of Christ to God suggested polytheism. The orthodox theologians proposed a statement that in philosophical language clarified the single substance of God, the one divine nature. The I.C.E.T. translation renders the lines about Christ with the following words:

> eternally begotten of the Father,
> God from God, Light from Light,
> true God from true God,
> begotten, not made,
> of one Being with the Father.

For decades this creed was defended by Athanasius, and it was further developed at the Council of Constantinople in 381, when the trinitarian work of the Cappadocians — Basil the Great, Gregory of Nazianzus, and Gregory of Nyssa — combated heresies that suggested two distinct Christs and that denigrated the person of the Spirit. At the Council of Chalcedon in 451 the creed was given its present form, except for the controverted *filioque,* the West's assertion, added a century later, that the Spirit proceeds from the Father "and the Son."

These christological controversies, carried out in different languages and thus different philosophical categories, sought to understand the scattered New Testament references about Father, Son, and Spirit and eventually structured Christian faith according to trinitarian beliefs. The Nicene Creed proposes verbs, "begotten" and "proceeding," to state the relationship of the Son and the Spirit to the Father. It orders the biblical witness concerning creation, incarnation, salvation, sanctification, and eschatology into three coherent paragraphs. It maintains forcefully that Christ is not less than God but is of one being with the Father, and it understands the life of the Spirit to be demonstrated in the present and future life of the Church. The Greek says there is one *ousia;* Latin says one *substantia:* one being of God, one God. There are three *hypostases* in Greek, three *personae* in Latin: three ways of the being. Our word "person" as a translation of *hypostasis* fortunately does not appear in the creed, for in the psychological movement of the last century the word has acquired connotations of individual personality that would muddle Gregory of Nyssa's philosophical point.

In reciting the creed we affirm our place in the Church catholic. Our assembly is not merely this congregation, but it includes the saints of time past who in their own language struggled for the meaning of Christian metaphors. If the Apostles' Creed calls up images of adult conversion and baptism, the Nicene Creed evokes pictures of an assembly of bishops and theologians debating for 125 years on the meaning of the faith. It is appropriate that the simple "holy catholic church" of the Apostles' Creed has become a full sentence: "We believe in one holy catholic and apostolic church." The councils believed that in their speech they were restating the faith of the apostles. We do the same, by reciting this document, central to our understanding, a vehicle of divine truth, yet an example of the very human process through which God is revealed. Various attempts in the Church to suppress the ecumenical creeds for containing too much unbiblical language are mistaken in their efforts to freeze biblical metaphors. The metaphors of faith are alive. They move around enthusiastically, demanding clarification in every time and every tongue.

THE ASSEMBLY AND THE LECTIONARY

Our ordinary liturgical texts have enough imagery to keep us probing the spiritual life all our days. We have also the three-year lectionary. We read in Matthew, Mark, and Luke in successive years. John is proclaimed on certain occasions throughout each cycle, especially in Lent and at Eastertide. The lectionary, the list of biblical readings judged significant for the assembly's consideration, is a gift to the whole assembly for its growth in the language of faith. The lectionary is culled from the entire canon, which itself is the collection of books judged appropriate for reading in the assembly. There are other ancient writings of Israel and other gospels of Jesus. Even the Bible itself has sections of only slight interest. In contrast, the pericopes of the three-year lectionary are the schoolhouse for the language of faith, all the diet we need. We hear again the poems and the prophecies, the stories and the sermons that gave birth to the language of the liturgy, and always the biblical texts are held in tension with the gospel so that Christ is proclaimed.

The point of the lectionary readings is not to take a walk through the Bible. The point is to proclaim the mystery of Christ, promised in the Old Testament, narrated in the Gospels, preached in the epistles, experienced in the liturgy, and hoped for in the eschaton. The history of the ancient Near East and the detailed biography of Jesus do not concern us. We attend the death and resurrection of Christ seen through the biblical narrative and in our local situation. Always we look for Christ in the Scriptures, Christ in the assembly, and Christ in the world's future. In Advent, then, we read of Israel's expectation of a messiah. We prepare ourselves for the arrival of a baby and a king. We anticipate the complete reign of God for which our lives are spent. We receive Christ in word, bread, and wine, coming as paradoxically to us as the Messiah came to Israel in Mary's womb. At Christmas we laud the incarnation, the birth of Christ who came to die. We celebrate God's presence in the liturgy. We pray for the birth of God's justice throughout the world. During the Epiphany season we read of the manifestation of the Spirit in the life of Jesus. We discover the same Spirit in our baptism and in our anointed lives. We look for the final transfiguration of this world's frailty into holiness by the vision of God.

Always it is the body of Christ we attend. That Jesus who was raised from the dead is the same Christ alive in the assembly, the same Lord for whose ultimate vindication we plead. We see this pattern of interpretation in the classic Johannine Lenten gospels, originally used as catechetical texts for the adults for whom Lent was

152

baptismal preparation.[4] John 4, 9, and 11 appear now in cycle A of Lent. These Lenten texts deal not with the sorrows of Jesus but with the gospel of Christ then, now, and to come. John 4, the narrative of the woman at the well, tells of Jesus' salvation brought to the Samaritan outsiders. Jesus' conversation about living water provided the Church with one of its primary metaphors for baptism. So in our baptism Christ offers us himself as living water, so that we, like the fallen woman, become witnesses of God's revelation to the world. John 9 is the narrative of Jesus' healing of the man born blind. The Church saw us all in this lively tale of surprise, anger, and evasion: we, like the blind man, need enlightenment from Christ. So Christ becomes our light, our baptismal candle, the paschal candle standing by the font. And we also are to be lights in the world, helping to enlighten the world with grace. John 11, the narrative of the raising of Lazarus, gave the Church a third metaphor for baptism: that of new life. So as Jesus raised the dead Lazarus to new life, we too are pulled out of our grave by the baptismal waters. Lazarus's white shroud becomes our baptismal robe, as we stand up alive in the presence of Christ, answering his call.

From these pericopes come our three main metaphors for baptism: living water, enlightenment, and new life. We hear them in Lent in order to recall our own baptism and to probe deeper into its meaning for our lives and for the world. The Old Testament lessons also show forth Christ and instruct us in liturgical language. When we read the story of the blind man anointed with Jesus' spittle and given sight, we read 1 Samuel 16, the anointing of the boy David to be king. So we too are anointed with oil to reign in God's dominion; we too are anointed by Jesus to see the glory of God. When we read the raising of Lazarus, we read Ezekiel 37, the valley of the dry bones. We are dried up, disconnected bones, dead and shrouded in sin; but we rise from our graves as God's new people, standing alive with the Spirit of Christ.

The lectionary moves us in time from Advent through Pentecost. On one level we go through the life of Jesus. But more significant, we travel each year again from the first coming of Christ at Bethlehem to the last coming in the eschaton by means of his continuous coming in the liturgy. The paschal cycle celebrates his death and our faith in the resurrection. The resurrection is imaged in various ways: the empty tomb of Easter, Jesus' disappearance in the skies at the ascension, the coming of the Spirit on Pentecost, and the feast of the Lamb at the end time. The Pentecost season explores the meaning of these comings and culminates in the festival of Christ the King. The lessons of Christ the King expound the metaphor of Christ's reign by telling the stories of the last judgment (Matthew 25:31-46), the conversation with Pilate about kingship (John 18:33-37), and the sign on the cross that read, "This is the King of the Jews" (Luke 23:35-43). The liturgical year concludes with Christ the King crucified; but the following Sunday, the first Sunday in Advent, reintroduces the hope for the coming of the king who will bring life to the world. For the king on the cross and the king in the manger are one and the same. The year's end and its beginning cast an evening and a morning light on the metaphor of God's reign to deepen further our sacred speech.

THE PREACHER: THE LITURGICAL HOMILY

Various types of sermons are represented by different denominations and preaching traditions. Calls to conversion fill up radio and television programs. Some commentaries on the biblical texts speculate on biographical or psychological detail, how tired Jesus was or what Judas' remorse was like. Theological expositions lay out intellectual categories by which the mysteries of God can be handled. Encouragement for the ethical life can direct the faithful to specific moral action or can deal more generally with growth in grace as ethical improvement. Topical preaching turns the sermon into a lecture, an address based on a topic perhaps suggested by the lessons or constituting part of the series. Recent recognition of biblical narrative as story has popularized the sermon as the preacher's story, an update on the preacher's spiritual journey as a spur to the hearer's own

self-examination and interior maturity. Hoping to rein
the sermon in more tightly to the lessons and away from
autobiography, liturgical reformers have urged that the
best vehicle for the proclamation of the gospel is the
liturgical homily.[5] This has come to mean a sermon based
directly on the lessons and conscious of its place in the
eucharistic assembly.

No matter what type, the sermon participates in
sacred speech. Of course, a truly bad sermon can be
dismissed as having so missed the mark as no longer to
fall within the range of sacred speech. But a sermon that
proclaims the Gospel, in whatever manner, is a verbal
event that uses biblical and traditional sacred speech in
such a way that the faithful assembly hears and receives
Christ anew. Sermons shape the word specifically to the
situation so that God's grace is encountered as astonishing surprise, the gift of life *pro me.* The homily is not to
be a soapbox for opinions or confessions too specific to
the preacher. Rather, while being based solidly in the
language of faith, the homily invites the assembly into
living in the faith more fully, so that the people can say,
"Amen!" The liturgical homily uses Christian sacred
speech in new combinations. Through the homily we
practice the language of faith. We fit biblical images
about God, Christ, the assembly, and the world into
contemporary sentences. The Word is incarnate in
current words.

The liturgical homily is usually understood as an
explication of the Gospel reading. In preparation the
preacher asks, What are the key words and images in
today's reading of the Gospel? What did these words
mean then? What do they mean now? How should they
best be translated? When we speak these words, how is
our life's vocabulary altered? What kind of folk would
we be were these words to become essential words in our
everyday speech? The homily applies a certain image of
God and a specific description of grace to the present
situation. Never a trivial thing, the homily yet stands
subservient to the language of faith.

But there has been more than one reading. In the
Roman lectionary's principle, followed in the Episcopal

and Lutheran lectionaries and often in the Consultation on Common Texts' lectionary, the Old Testament lesson is chosen to complement the Gospel reading. Following the primitive Christian pattern, this practice assumes that Christians read the Hebrew Scriptures mainly because also in them Christ is proclaimed. Christ was raised "in accordance with the scriptures," writes Paul (1 Corinthians 15:4), meaning of course the Hebrew Scriptures. If studying the Gospel reading is the preacher's first task in preparation, exploring the complementarity of the first to the third lesson is the second task. Sometimes the lessons give similar stories of God's grace: on the Sunday that we read of God's miraculous feeding of Israel with quail (Exodus 16:2-15), Christ says of all miraculous feedings, "I am the bread of life" (John 6:24-35). Sometimes the images are contrasting: the ancient myth of the great tree of life (Ezekiel 17:22-24) accentuates the paradox of Jesus' parable about the mustard bush (Mark 4:30-32). Other times the church's skill of typological interpretation illuminates the Old Testament with its christological vision: on Good Friday Christians read the suffering-servant poems of Isaiah as if they refer to Jesus of Nazareth crucified, and at the Easter Vigil we read the exodus account at if it were about baptism. A good liturgical homily capitalizes on the interplay between the first and third lessons in order to present a richer context for Christian sacred speech. The consummate liturgical preacher can also find a phrase or two in the second reading, even when the epistles are read in course, that offer their own nuance for the sacred speech of the day.

The liturgical homily is shaped by its position in the eucharistic liturgy. In the first place this means that the liturgical homily is shorter rather than longer. Since the key moments of the Eucharist are the reading of the lessons and the sharing of the bread and wine, the liturgical homily, as the commentary on the lessons, is not the focus of the liturgy and cannot by its length or style supersede the Eucharist itself.

The position of the homily within the eucharistic action places another obligation on the preacher. Twenty years ago, structural analysis of the eucharistic rite as a combination of synagogue and meal led to an understanding of the liturgy as two combined events. Some communities even designed their worship spaces with two areas, one for the readings and one for the meal. But played out to excess this recognition of the origins of the Christian eucharist forgets the essential truth that the reason Christians gather to sing praises, to hear the word, and to pray is to celebrate the risen Lord in bread and wine. We meet on the first day of the week to break the bread of the resurrection, and even as we read Hebrew narratives, we do so because of, and before, the table. Thus in late November, when the church reads of the final judgment, the preacher has not only to grapple with New Testament parables of good sheep and bad goats held next to Old Testament images of God as shepherd, but also to shine on these lessons the light of the cross and resurrection. The liturgical homily always takes place in the face of the bread and wine.

Thus the liturgical homily at its best is neither a commercial that breaks up the show nor the show surrounded by commercials. It is mystagogy, catechesis for the faithful, instruction in how this sacred speech and these holy symbols can be incorporated into contemporary life. The homily allows the preacher — presumably uniquely adept·or trained in this skill — to rehearse the sacred images, to try them out, to apply them, this Sunday, to yesterday's crisis or tomorrow's pain. The liturgical homily is called to be a school of sacred speech. Preachers are ordained to get their mouths around the mysteries of God and the paradox of the cross, and the baptized are invited then to rise in acclamation, saying amen, singing praises, reciting the creed, presenting bread and wine, and sharing the meal. Like foreigners in a new land, we need continually to learn more Christian sacred speech. If in the course of our worship we speak the sacred words often enough, our speech will grow closer to that of the angels. If we hear often enough Isaiah's call, "Come to the feast," our whole life will be enlivened by our meals with the risen Christ.

Second Thoughts

I cannot stress enough the enormity and the endless-
ness of the task of liturgical catechesis. It is not only that
many people in our society are biblically illiterate and
symbolically stunted. Many of our churches accentuate
the problems by, for example, offering Sunday school
during church services, imagining that two years of
instruction with young teens is sufficient for the confirmation of the faithful, or neglecting continuous adult
mystagogy. Liturgical instruction at all levels needs to
include not only the metaphors of the faith, but also the
method of how one comes to appropriate such metaphors
into thought and action.

Concerning *Abba*: Although scholars today are less
certain of the original meaning of *Abba* than Joachim
Jeremias was, it still provides a good prayer for parents to
say with infants. Some parents may wish to intersperse
Abba with *Imma*. By the time my daughters were
preschoolers, their evening prayer had matured from
"*Abba*, Amen" to include metaphoric method:

> Thank you, God, for being our father.
> Thank you, God, for being our mother.
> Thank you, God, for being our friend.
> Thank you, God, for being our castle.

One daughter used to ask for the prayer, and then
conclude it by saying, "God is not a castle: God is God."
It seemed to me that the method was working.

About the Lord's Prayer: The primary point of this
prayer, like that of other first-century Jewish prayers, is
to beg for the coming of God's dominion and to ask that
we be prepared to receive and enact its merciful surprises. The Lord's Prayer needs to stand next to the
Magnificat and so remember that God's will is quite
other than our own. I am glad to know what Cyril of
Jerusalem said of the phrase "our Father in heaven":
"They too are a heaven who bear the image of the heavenly,

in whom God is, dwelling and walking in them." Even "heaven" is other than we first thought. It is among us in the Spirit, rather than levitating somewhere in the clouds.

About the ecumenical creeds: The creed appointed for normal use in the Sunday liturgy is either the Apostles' Creed, the restatement of baptismal beliefs, or the Nicene Creed, an example of the Church's theological task to articulate its christological and trinitarian faith. Adult instruction about the origin and meaning of these creeds should be offered regularly in our parishes. *Quicunque Vult,* the so-called Athanasian Creed, is no longer liturgically useful and is best reserved solely for classroom instruction and discussion.

About newly-composed creeds: One or several individuals composing a contemporary creed is a temptation to be resisted. Expecting an assembly of persons who have never laid eyes on a creed to affirm it publicly offends their integrity. Rather, the entire church needs to work together on expressions of the faith that speak in the categories of the twenty-first century, rather than those of the fifth century. Most contemporary creeds that I have encountered are Arian in that they construe Christ as less than God, the very heresy that the Nicene Creed sought to address.

Concerning lectionaries: I wrote that the Scriptures as stipulated in the lectionary serve up "all the diet we need." This enthusiastic defense of the lectionary is, admittedly, an overstatement. I fiercely advocate that continuous and intense Bible study be conducted in every parish on every level and that daily Bible reading remain part of the religious life of faithful Christians. The lectionary selects out only a small portion of the Bible, and it is good if Christians know more of the Bible than any current lectionary system prescribes.

What I did mean by that statement is my conviction that the three-year lectionary is the best system that the church has yet devised for presenting before the baptized community those parts of the Bible attendant to Christian faith. My question about Bible readings on Sunday is: why should the faithful hear this particular reading? The Sunday readings, I assert, are chosen not because

they convey the preacher's favorite passages, or illustrate
the heights or depths of socio-economic history, or
exemplify what my honors English teacher called "the
wide truths of life," but rather because they proclaim the
Gospel to the eucharistic assembly. At least let us agree
that making these choices is not an easy task.

Concerning the three-year lectionary: I now teach
that the three synoptic Gospels circle around John,
which, despite its various problems, is the metaphoric
jewel of the New Testament. For example, let us examine
the chapters concerning Jesus' birth. Matthew's and
Luke's accounts of the birth of Christ present themselves
as historical narratives. Of course, the biblical scholar
knows well that Matthew did not have access to accurate
historical information, but rather intends to proclaim
that Jesus is the anointed king that God promised to send
to Israel. Similarly, Luke is not recording data, but proclaiming that Jesus comes to and among the poorest and
lowliest of God's people. John goes the further step: he
omits the narrative guise completely. In poetic form,
John presents the gospel that Christ is the Word of God,
the light of the world from creation until the end, and
the flesh of almighty God among us.

The lectionary acknowledges this difference in
genre. Appointed as the readings on Christmas Eve and
Epiphany, the narratives from Luke and Matthew enter-
tain and thus engage us. However, for the reading on
Christmas Day from John, the metaphors carry the
gospel. Do me a favor: follow the wisdom of the lectionary, and proclaim and preach John 1 to the few who
come to church on Christmas Day. Perhaps other persons
besides me have come eagerly anticipating the magnifi-
cence of the Johannine prologue.

Those of you who use the semi-continuous readings
from the Old Testament during the summer and autumn
Sundays have an exceptionally difficult task. Granting
that I understand the lectionary to provide the church
with a carefully-honed list of those biblical passages that
best proclaim resurrection faith to Christians, I prefer a
use of the Old Testament that ties together the faith of
God's ancient covenant people with the narratives of the

Gospels. In the semi-continuous readings, the stories of Israel hang loosely on a chronological frame in a "history" that scholars have shown to have been determined more by faith, legend and propaganda than by fact. Thus these stories are history only in a metaphoric way. The liturgical homilist must avoid commenting upon the vagaries of the ancient world and must rather hold these motley tales before the face of the bread and wine. I believe that the Christian liturgical use of the Bible is a specific use, with its own guidelines, strengths and, yes, weaknesses, and that the liturgical use of the Bible is different from its use as historical document, moral instruction, psychological wellspring or resource for a study of comparative religion. We need to reflect more intently than we have on how the Bible best functions as a liturgical text.

Concerning the word "typology": I now avoid this term, having discovered that people tend to associate it with a replacement theology, in which the history of Israel is viewed as a negative opposite of the positive life of Christ. I do not advocate a Christian use of the Hebrew Scriptures such that, for example, Mount Sinai is bad and the Sermon on the Mount good. Quite the contrary, I see God's mercy as revealed in Christ to be an extension of the divine grace that the community already experienced through the covenant. Since to many people the word typology suggests medieval anti-Semitic hermeneutical extremes, I talk instead of "parallel" biblical texts.

In the chapter I claim that the key moments of the liturgy are the reading of the word and the sharing of the bread and wine. Someone more Lutheran than I (can this be possible?!) said no, not the reading of the word, but its proclamation in the sermon. It is perhaps good for preachers to think this way. After fifty years of listening to sermons, however, I find that this elevated status for preaching is seldom realized.

I must add to the chapter a final consideration: The Building as Liturgical Proclamation.

It is incongruous that many churches which rely on metaphor and symbol to undergird and explicate their liturgy have in the last fifty years constructed their worship facilities on the model of the Quaker meeting house. For

Quakers, a plain room devoid of symbol makes complete theological sense. Since Quakers believe that the divine light resides in each individual, the weekly meeting provides the community with an unobscured access to other Friends. However, for sacramental Christians, a bare building makes no sense at all. Of course, some of this century's purging is the result of necessary housecleaning: many church buildings were or still are filled with sanctimonious junk. It may have been the meager depiction of the Trinity in the church of my childhood that accounts for my lifelong search for more liturgically evocative and theologically appropriate art in the church. Indeed, examining the art on church walls, windows, banners and bulletins, I can attest that successful, perhaps even profound, contemporary liturgical art is extremely difficult to locate.

Yet I have traveled to churches around the world where the entire interior of the building was dedicated to metaphoric instruction. Think of the icons surrounding an Eastern Orthodox assembly, or the frescos from the fifteenth century which depicted the entire life of Christ on the walls, with parallel stories from the Old Testament on the ceiling, and the saints on the pillars. Visit the church of Notre-Dame in Assy, France, where Marc Chagall's mural of the Israelites crossing the Red Sea manifests the meaning of the baptistry. What if we designed the church art on one wall to depict all the biblical stories of hearing the word (Moses and the burning bush, for example, and the woman at the well) and on the opposite wall all the stories about eating with God and one another? Or what if around the room we presented the stories from both Old and New Testaments that illumine the liturgical year? Can we design and decorate our worship spaces so that they embrace the faithful with liturgical metaphor? When I see new stained glass windows that are merely nonrepresentational splays of color, I grieve for the loss of an opportunity to form the faithful into God's people.

CONCLUSION

We began our analysis of liturgical language aware that the words themselves must be broken. Christ is the Lamb; but Christ is not a lamb! Yet we say, Christ is the Lamb. YES, NO, YES. The words are not what they seem. As metaphor the words are not mere labels. They are harbingers of the resurrection, signs of life seen anew. But our realization that even our most carefully chosen words cannot grasp God, that our words are finally inadequate for praise, leads us to liturgical silence.

Religious mysticism, realizing the failure of language, develops nonverbal vehicles for praise and prayer. Hoping for direct nonverbal communication with God, the mystic is propelled beyond time and place, where words are unnecessary for human expression and divine revelation. But Christian worship is always communal. Even the individual at prayer is a part of the community. When praying alone, we pray the words of the Christian assembly and we learn from centuries of Christians what those words mean. Because Christian worship is communal, some words must be used, and our most fundamental description of God that God speaks indicates faith in a God whose saving will can be expressed in human language.

Christian silence is not a religious mysticism that forgoes words. Christian silence is the moment after words, the time of awe at the revelation. Christian silence is Mary, quietly pondering in her heart the words of her son. Christian silence is Mary of Bethany, sitting attentively at Jesus' feet while he pauses for a breath. The Hebrew Scriptures speak of our awe in the holy place, our keeping silence in the Lord's temple (Habakkuk 2:20). But in the incarnation God has moved out of the Most Holy Place and into a stable, up onto a cross. These words strike us mute. With old Zechariah we have heard the angel's promise and we are struck

163

silent for a time. Christian silence is the moment of
meditation after the hearing of the sacred speech; as if in
the silence we can travel up the words, through the
words, into the very silence of God. So some Christians
keep silence after the Gospel, the homily, or the communion. Christian silence is not only the minutes given
us to think about the words, the time to reflect on the
layers of denotations and connotations of our complex
Christian vocabulary. Christian silence is meditation
beyond the words, when finally granting all our biblical
exegesis and metaphoric interpretation, we rest, and like
Jacob asleep, allow God to come down the ladder into
our quiet space and bless us.

Christian contemplation provides the last interpretive layer to liturgical language, the awe of silence before
God revealed in Christ the Word. Full Christian liturgical
expression requires not only the biblical expertise of
Jerome, the liturgical life of Benedict, the theological
study of Dominic, the concern for the poor of Francis,
and the ecstasy of Catherine; it requires also the silence
of Bernard of Clairvaux. In a hymn by Bernard translated
"O Jesus, Joy of Loving Hearts" is the following stanza:

> We taste you, ever-living Bread,
> And long to feast upon you still;
> We drink of you, the Fountainhead;
> Our thirsting souls from you we fill.[1]

This contemplative knew well the metaphoric use of
language taught in the church and enacted in the assembly. But in their daily prayer Bernard's Cistercians would
keep silence after these rich metaphors, first in contemplation of the metaphors, but then as if carried by the
strength of the metaphors beyond language itself, in
contemplation of the wordless mystery of God.

Christian silence is an acknowledgments that our
words about God are not, finally, the actual being of God.
Our assembly contains the words, but even the heavens
and earth cannot contain God. The mystery of Christian
worship is that in our sacred speech, in our little bread
and wine, God chooses to be revealed. But our liturgy

does not contain all there is of God. Perhaps, in speaking of Christ, our liturgical language conveys all of God that we can bear. But there is far more, and hearing those words about God is part of our hope of heaven.

CONCLUDING THOUGHTS

I concluded *Christ in Sacred Speech* with the word "heaven." I am more careful with that word now than I used to be. What does "heaven" mean? On this Christians do not agree. Some say heaven is a literal place, a perpetual embodied life after death for the good guys or, perhaps, for nearly everyone. Some say the word names some sort of existence with God, to which all life returns. Some say the word is a metaphor for things divine, a kind of synecdoche for the deity; "heaven" a way to dress up the sentence, to enlarge our speech, when we say "God." Fortunately the liturgy does not require us to vote on this question. The word is wide enough for all these Christians together to walk alongside one another.

I think of chapter 51 in the writings of Julian of Norwich, as she struggled with the liturgical phrase that "the Son sits at the right hand of the Father." As her fifteenth-century English has it, "But it is not ment that the Son syttith on the ryte hond, syde by syde, as on man sittith be another in this lif; for there is no such sytting, as to my syte, in the Trinite." "Right hand," Julian decides, means "right in the highest nobility of the Father's joy."

I like her line "no such sitting in the Trinity." Yet she, and we all, continue to use the image of God's right hand in the *Gloria in Excelsis*, in the creeds, on Ascension Day, in preaching. We are not sure what the metaphor means, but then there is little about the life of God that our language can make clear. I hope that after we say such a phrase, we keep silence for a moment, reaching out through the metaphor into the life of the Trinity, ready to receive that abundant life as it pours out all around us, and together living in this world in such a way that we reflect that "highest nobility" of the joy of God.

But finally, were I now concluding this book, I would not do so with a discussion of silence. Fifteen years ago I was closer than I am now to Cistercian spirituality, having recently completed a dissertation on the Trappist Thomas Merton. Yes, Christian worship needs silence, considerably more than most assemblies grant it — as do, indeed, our lives — silence after each reading, after the preaching, after the communion.

But liturgical metaphors, after a moment of awestruck hush, burst forth into yet more metaphors. So to end this study of liturgical metaphor, I conclude with cacophony. I think of the great multitude, the angels, and the four living creatures who are singing "Amen! Blessing and glory and wisdom and thanksgiving and honor and power and might be to our God forever and ever! Amen!" I join with the countless suffering ones who cry out Psalm 44 to God, "Awake! Why are you sleeping?" (Can you hear how loud is their clamor?) I listen for all the trees of the wood shouting for joy, since God is coming to bring justice to the earth. We speak as if God were a lamb on a throne, as if God were sometimes sound asleep, as if the trees could sing their praises: metaphors, metaphors.

All this numinous tumult would lead me, not to quiet contemplation, but to yet more sacred speech, to something perhaps like this:

Our God, our Mercy, our Might,
  Our Table, our Food, our Server,
    Our Rainbow, our Ark, our Dove,
Our Sovereign, our Water, our Wine,
  Our Way, our Truth, our Life,
    Our Light, our Treasure, our Tree:
Praise, Holy God, Holy One, Holy Three.
Amen.

If biblical images are only like old photographs, they will fade away. But I say that the images can live. All these liturgical metaphors can bud and flower. Each thriving metaphor encourages another. Yet this revitalization will not happen miraculously: there will be no "spontaneous generation." Reviving our sacred speech is a perpetual responsibility of all of us in the Church. The tree must be tended and watered and pruned: let's help one another each week with this continual undertaking. The tree is burning with God: let's get as close to it as we can.

NOTES

Chapter 1

1. Gerardus van der Leeuw, *Sacred and Profane Beauty,* part 3: "Beautiful Words," trans. David E. Green (Nashville: Abingdon Press, 1963), 115-18.
2. Cyril of Jerusalem, *Lectures on the Christian Sacraments,* ed. F. L. Cross (Crestwood, N.Y.: St. Vladimir's Seminary Press, 1977). See also Aidan Kavanagh, *On Liturgical Theology* (New York: Pueblo Pub. Co., 1984); Robert W. Jenson, *Visible Words* (Philadelphia: Fortress Press, 1978); Alexander Schmemann, *Introduction to Liturgical Theology,* trans. Asheleigh E. Moorhouse (Portland, Me.: American Orthodox Press, 1966); Geoffrey Wainwright, *Doxology* (New York: Oxford Univ. Press, 1980).
3. Gerhard Ebeling, *Introduction to a Theological Theory of Language,* trans. R. A. Wilson (London: William Collins Sons, 1973), 191.
4. See, e.g., I. A. Richards, *The Philosophy of Rhetoric* (New York: Oxford Univ. Press, 1981); and Paul Ricoeur, *The Rule of Metaphor,* trans. Robert Czerny (Toronto: Univ. of Toronto Press, 1977).
5. C. G. Jung, *Psychology and Religion* (New Haven: Yale Univ. Press, 1938), 49.
6. Marion J. Hatchett, *Commentary on the American Prayer Book* (New York: Seabury Press, 1980), 174, 185.
7. Northrop Frye, *The Great Code* (New York: Harcourt Brace Jovanovich, 1982), 15.
8. J. L. Austin, *How to Do Things with Words* (Oxford: Clarendon Press, 1962), 151-64.
9. See, e.g., Donald Evans, *The Logic of Self-Involvement* (New York: Herder & Herder, 1969); A. C. Thiselton, *Language, Liturgy, and Meaning,* Grove Liturgical Study 2 (Bromcote, Nottinghamshire, England: Grove Books, 1975); and James H. Ware, Jr., *Not with Words of Wisdom* (Washington, D.C.: Univ. Press of America, 1981).
10. Paul Ricoeur, *The Symbolism of Evil,* trans. Emerson Buchanan (New York: Harper & Row, 1967), and idem, *The Rule of Metaphor.*

11. See, e.g., Ernst Cassirer, *Language and Myth,* trans. Susanne K. Langer (New York: Dover, 1946); Max Black, *Models and Metaphors* (Ithaca, N.Y.: Cornell Univ. Press, 1962); and Philip Wheelwright, *The Burning Fountain* (Bloomington: Ind. Univ. Press, 1968).

12. Thomas Aquinas, "Question 13," *Summa Theologiae,* la.l3.1-12 (London: Blackfriars, 1963), 67-71.

13. Nelson Goodman, *Languages of Art* (Indianapolis: Bobbs-Merrill, 1968), 69.

14. See, e.g., Sallie McFague, *Metaphorical Theology* (Philadelphia: Fortress Press, 1982); Norman Perrin, *Jesus and the Language of the Kingdom* (Philadelphia: Fortress Press, 1976); David N. Power, *Unsearchable Riches* (New York: Pueblo Pub. Co., 1984); Phyllis Trible, *God and the Rhetoric of Sexuality* (Philadelphia: Fortress Press, 1978); and Amos Niven Wilder, *Theopoetic* (Philadelphia: Fortress Press, 1976).

15. Daniel Stevick, "The Language of Prayer," *Worship* 52 (1978): 547.

Chapter 2

1. Rudolf Otto, *The Idea of the Holy,* trans. John W. Harvey (New York: Oxford Univ. Press, 1952), 7.

2. See, e.g., Mircea Eliade, *The Sacred and the Profane,* trans. Willard Trask (New York: Harcourt, Brace & Co., 1959); C. G. Jung, *Modern Man in Search of a Soul* (New York: Harcourt, Brace & Co., 1939); and Clifford Geertz, "Religion as a Cultural System," in his *The Interpretation of Cultures* (New York: Basic Books, 1973).

3. Don Saliers, *The Soul in Paraphrase* (Akron: OSL Publications, 1995), 11.

4. Edward Schillebeeckx, *Interim Report on the Books Jesus and Christ* (New York: Crossroad, 1981), 23-24.

5. Dietrich Bonhoeffer, *Psalms: The Prayer Book of the Church,* trans. James H. Burtness (Minneapolis: Augsburg Pub. House, 1970), 14-15.

6. Mary Gerhard and Allan Russell, *Metaphoric Process* (Fort Worth: Tex. Christian Univ. Press, 1984), 114.

Chapter 3

1. Pseudo-Dionysius Areopagite, *The Divine Names and Mystical Theology,* trans. John D. Jones (Milwaukee: Marquette Univ. Press, 1980), 221-22.

2. Meister Eckhard, "Sermon 83," in *The Essential Sermons, Commentaries, Treatises, and Defense,* trans. and intro. Edmund Colledge, O.S.A., and Bernard McGinn (New York: Paulist Press, 1981), 206-7.

3. Catherine of Siena, *The Dialogue,* trans. and intro. Suzanne Noffke, O.P. (New York: Paulist Press, 1980), 325.

4. Dante Alighieri, *Paradise,* trans. Dorothy L. Sayers and Barbara Reynolds (New York: Penguin Books, 1962), 346.

5. Augustine, "On Christian Doctrine," in *A Select Library of the Nicene and Post-Nicene Fathers of the Christian Church,* vol. 2, ed. Philip Schaff (Grand Rapids: Wm. B. Eerdmans, 1979), 524.

6. James A. Weisheipl, O.P., *Friar Thomas D'Aquino: His Life, Thought, and Work* (Garden City, N.Y.: Doubleday & Co., 1974), 322.

7. See, e.g., Gordon D. Kaufman, *God the Problem* (Cambridge: Harvard Univ. Press, 1972), 84- 86; Hans Urs von Balthasar, "The Unknown God," in *The von Balthasar Reader,* ed. Medard Kehl, S.J., and Werner Loser, S.J., trans. Robert H. Daly, S.J., and Fred Lawrence (New York: Crossroad, 1982), 181-87.

8. Juliana of Norwich, *Revelations of Divine Love,* trans. and intro. M. L. Del Mastro (Garden City, N. Y.: Doubleday & Co., 1971), 191.

9. Robert W. Jenson, *Triune Identity* (Philadelphia: Fortress Press, 1982), 16-18.

10. Paul Ricoeur, *The Rule of Metaphor,* trans. Robert Czemy (Toronto: Univ. of Toronto Press, 1977), 224.

11. Anselm, "Proslogion," in *A Scholastic Miscellany: Anselm to Ockham,* Library of Christian Classics 10, ed. and trans. Eugene R. Fairweather (Philadelphia: Westminster Press, 1961), 73.

12. Tertullian, "On the Flesh of Christ," in *The Ante-Nicene Fathers,* vol.3, ed. Alexander Robert and James Donaldson (Grand Rapids: Wm. B. Eerdmans, 1978), 525.

Chapter 4

1. Joachim Jeremias, *The Prayers of Jesus,* trans. John Bowden et al. (Philadelphia: Fortress Press, 1978), 58. That "Abba" was not unique to Jesus is seen in Asher Finkel, "The Prayer of Jesus in Matthew, " in *Standing Before God,* ed. Asher Finkel and Lawrence Frizzell (New York: Ktav Pub. House, 1981), 155-58.

2. Rosemary Radford Ruether, *Sexism and God-Talk* (Boston: Beacon Press, 1983), 45-46.

3. Division of Education and Ministry, National Council of Churches of Christ, *An Inclusive Language Lectionary: Readings for Year A* (Philadelphia: Westminster Press, 1983), appendix, no page.

4. Irenaeus, "Against Heresies," in *Early Christian Fathers,* Library of Christian Classics 1, trans. and ed. Cyril C. Richardson (Philadelphia: Westminster Press, 1953), 358-60.

5. Gregory of Nyssa, "An Answer to Ablabius: That We Should Not Think of Saying There Are Three Gods," in *Christology of the Later Fathers,* Library of Christian Classics 3, ed. and trans. Edward R. Hardy and Cyril C. Richardson (Philadelphia: Westminster Press, 1954), 261-64.

6. Martin Luther, "Large Catechism," in *The Book of Concord,* ed. Theodore G. Tappert (Philadelphia: Muhlenberg Press, 1959), 422-23.

7. Sigmund Freud, *Civilization and Its Discontents,* trans. James Strachey (New York: W. W. Norton & Co., 1961), 21.

8. Ruether, *Sexism and God-Talk,* 53-54, 122-26.

9. Antoine Vergote and Catherine Aubert, "Parental Images and Representations of God," trans. Jean Houard, *Social Compass 19*(1972): 443.

10. Brother Roger, *Praying Together in Word and Song* (Oxford: A. R. Mowbray & Co., 1982), 4, 14-16.

11. Josef Jungmann, S.J., *The Place of Christ in Liturgical Prayer,* trans. A. Peeler (Staten Island, N.Y.: Alba House, 1965), 192.

12. J. N. D. Kelly, *Early Christian Doctrines,* 2d ed. (New York: Harper & Row, 1960), 226-31, 310-17.

13. Thomas Jefferson, *The Jefferson Bible* (New York: Grosset & Dunlap, 1940).

14. Mary Daly, *Beyond God the Father* (Boston: Beacon Press, 1973), and idem, *Gyn/ecology* (Boston: Beacon Press, 1978).

15. See, e.g., Leonard Swidler, "God the Father: Masculine; God the Son: Masculine; God the Holy Spirit: Feminine," *National Catholic Reporter,* January 31, 1975, 7, 14.

16. Elizabeth A. Johnson, C.S.J., "The Incomprehensibility of God and the Image of God Male and Female," *Theological Studies* 45 (1984): 458-60.

17. Kelly, *Early Christian Doctrines,* 264-67; and Robert W. Jenson, *Triune Identity* (Philadelphia: Fortress Press, 1982), 103-11.

18. Gordon W. Lathrop, "The Prayers of Jesus and the Great Prayer of the Church," *Lutheran Quarterly* 26 (1974): 172.
19. "The Eucharistic Liturgy of Lima," in *Baptism and Eucharist: Ecumenical Convergence in Celebration,* ed. Max Thurian and Geoffrey Wainwright (Grand Rapids: Wm. B. Eerdmans, 1983), 249 -55.
20. *Inclusive Language Guidelines for Use and Study in the United Church of Christ,* June 1980, 6.
21. Leonid Ouspensky and Vladimir Lossky, *The Meaning of Icons,* trans. G. E. H. Palmer and E. Kadloubovsky (Crestwood, N.Y.: St. Vladimir's Seminary Press, 1982), 204.
22. Martin Luther, "The German Mass and Order of Service, 1526," in *Liturgy and Hymns,* vol. 53 of *Luther's Works,* ed. Ulrich S. Leupold (Philadelphia: Fortress Press, 1965), 84.

Chapter 5

1. Raymond E. Brown, S.S., *The Gospel According to John,* Anchor Bible 29 (Garden City, N.Y.: Doubleday & Co., 1966), 58-63.
2. Translations of "Veni Creator Spiritus" are found in *The Hymnal 1982* (New York: Church Pension Fund, 1985), no. 503, and in *Lutheran Book of Worship* (Philadelphia: Board of Pub. Lutheran Church in America, 1978), no. 472, "Come, Holy Ghost, our souls inspire"; and in *Worship II* (Chicago: G.I.A. Pubs., 1975), no. 50, "Come, Holy Ghost, Creator blest." Translations of "Veni Sancte Spiritus" are found in *The Hymnal 1982,* no. 226; and in *Worship II,* no. 56, "Come, thou Holy Spirit"; and in *Service Book and Hymnal* (Philadelphia: Board of Pub., Lutheran Church in America, 1958), no. 121, "Come, Holy Ghost, in love." Other translations of both hymns can be found in other hymnals.
3. Rosemary Radford Ruether, *Sexism and God-Talk* (Boston: Beacon Press, 1983).
4. Mary Daly, *Gyn/ecology* (Boston: Beacon Press, 1978).
5. Letty M. Russell, ed., *Feminist Interpretation of the Bible* (Philadelphia: Westminster Press, 1985), and Elisabeth Schussler Fiorenza, *Bread Not Stone* (Boston: Beacon Press, 1984).
6. See, e.g., Elisabeth Schussler Fiorenza, *In Memory of Her* (New York: Crossroad, 1983); Caroline Walker Bynum, *Jesus as Mother* (Berkeley: Univ. of Calif. Press, 1982); and Patricia Wilson-Kastner, *Faith, Feminism, and the Christ* (Philadelphia: Fortress Press, 1983).

7. See the psalm translations in *Consultation on a Liturgical Psalter* (Washington, D.C.: International Commission on English in the Liturgy, 1984), and *The Psalms: A New Translation for Prayer and Worship,* trans. Gary Chamberlain (Nashville: The Upper Room, 1984).

8. See, e.g., Jane Parker Huber, *Joy in Singing* (The Joint Office of Women and the Joint Office of Worship, Presbyterian Church U.S.A., 1983.)

9. Nowhere in this book is "he" or "his" used to refer to God.

Chapter 6

1. Adolf Adam, *The Liturgical Year,* trans. Matthew J. O'Connell (New York: Pueblo Pub. Co., 1981), 40.

2. Mircea Eliade, *The Sacred and the Profane,* trans. Willard Trask (New York: Harcourt, Brace & Co., 1959), 70-72.

3. Odo Casel, *The Mystery of Christian Worship,* ed. Burkhard Neunhauser (Westminster, Md.: Newman Press, 1962), 63-93.

4. For a full discussion of Sunday, see Willy Rordorf, *Sunday* (London: SCM Press, 1986).

5. Justin Martyr, "First Apology," 67.7, in *Prayers of the Eucharist, Early and Reformed,* 2d ed., R. C. D. Jasper and G. J. Cuming (New York: Oxford Univ. Press, 1980), 20.

6. Adam, *The Liturgical Year,* 43.

7. Gordon Lathrop, "Words at the Solstice, " *Dialog* 21 (1982): 247-52.

8. Translations of the *Exsultet* are found in *The Book of Common Prayer* (New York: Seabury Press, 1979), 286- 87; *From Ashes to Fire,* Supplemental Worship Resources 8 (Nashville: Abingdon Press, 1979), 170-72; *Lutheran Book of Worship, Ministers Desk Edition* (Philadelphia: Board of Pub., Lutheran Church in America, 1978), 144-46; and *The Sacramentary* (Collegeville, Minn.: Liturgical Press, 1974), 241-42.

9. *Inclusive Language Guidelines for Use and Study in the United Church of Christ,* June 1980, 6.

10. *The Oxford Book of Carols* (London: Oxford Univ. Press, 1964), no. 180.

11. David N. Power, "Words That Crack: The Uses of 'Sacrifice' in Eucharistic Discourse," *Worship* 53 (1979): 385-404.

12. *The Liturgy of the Hours,* International Commission on English in the Liturgy, 4 vols. (New York: Catholic Book Pub. Co., 1975).

13. See translation by Catherine Winkworth, altered, in *Lutheran Book of Worship* (Philadelphia: Board of Pub., Lutheran Church in America, 1978), no. 31.

Chapter 7

1. See articles in *Liturgy: Holy Places* 3 (1983).
2. James F. White, *Introduction to Christian Worship* (Nashville: Abingdon Press, 1980), 84-97.
3. Frederic Debuyst, *Modern Architecture and Christian Celebration,* Ecumenical Studies in Worship 18 (London: Lutterworth Press, 1968).
4. "Constitutions of the Holy Apostles," in *The Ante-Nicene Fathers,* vol. 7, ed. Alexander Roberts and James Donaldson (Grand Rapids: Wm. B. Eerdmans, 1979), 421.

Chapter 8

1. Hippolytus, "The Apostolic Tradition," in *Prayers of the Eucharist, Early and Reformed,* 2d ed., ed. R. C. D. Jasper and G. J. Cuming (New York: Oxford Univ. Press, 1980), 23-25.
2. Mircea Eliade, *Patterns in Comparative Religion,* trans. Rosemary Sheed (New York: New American Library, 1963), 19-23.
3. John Matthews, *The Grail* (New York: Crossroad, 1981).
4. Hippolytus, "Apostolic Tradition," 23.
5. Edward Schillebeeckx, O.P., *The Eucharist,* trans. N. D. Smith (New York: Sheed & Ward, 1968).
6. Robert H. Daly, S.J., *Christian Sacrifice* (Washington, D.C.: Catholic Univ. of America Press, 1978), 77, 140-41, 498-508; versus David N. Power, "Words That Crack: The Uses of 'Sacrifice' in Eucharistic Discourse," *Worship* 53 (1979): 388-89.
7. James F. White, *Introduction to Christian Worship* (Nashville: Abingdon Press, 1980), 83.
8. For prayers of thanksgiving over the baptismal waters, see *The Book of Common Prayer* (New York: Seabury Press, 1979), 306-7; *Lutheran Book of Worship* (Philadelphia: Board of America, 1978), 122; *The Rites of the Catholic Church* (New York: Pueblo Pub. Co., 1976), 96-98; and A *Service of Baptism, Confirmation, and Renewal,* rev. ed., Supplemental Worship Resources 2 (Nashville: Parthenon Press, 1980), 16- 17.
9. J. G. Davies, *The Architectural Setting of Baptism* (London: Barrie & Rocklift, 1962), 80-87.

Chapter 9

1. Thomas Merton, "Day of a Stranger," in A *Thomas Merton Reader,* ed. Thomas McDonnell (Garden City, N.Y.: Doubleday & Co., 1974), 431.
2. "The Holy Eucharist II," *Worship Supplement* (St. Louis: Concordia Pub. House, 1969), 59.
3. *Presidential Prayers for Experimental Use at Mass* (Washington, D.C.: International Commission on English in the Liturgy, 1983), 38.
4. Sharon Neufer Emswiler and Thomas Neufer Emswiler, *Women and Worship,* rev. ed. (San Francisco: Harper & Row, 1984).
5. Erik H. Erikson, *Identity: Youth and Crisis* (New York: W. W. Norton & Co., 1968), 15-19.
6. For prayers invoking the Holy Spirit, see *The Book of Common Prayer* (New York: Seabury Press, 1979), 308, 309; *The Lutheran Book of Worship* (Philadelphia: Board of Pub., Lutheran Church in America, 1978), 124, 201; and *The Rites of the Catholic Church* (New York: Pueblo Pub. Co., 1976), 103-4, 309.
7. Martin Luther, *Lectures on Romans,* vol. 25 of *Luther's Works,* ed. Hilton C. Oswald (St. Louis: Concordia Pub. House, 1972), 63, 260.
8. Justin Martyr, "First Apology," in *Prayers of the Eucharist, Early and Reformed,* 2d ed., ed. R. C. D. Jasper and G. J. Cuming (New York: Oxford Univ. Press, 1980), 20.
9. Raymond E. Brown et al., *Mary in the New Testament* (Philadelphia: Fortress Press, 1978); Thomas A. O'Meara, O.P., *Mary in Protestant and Catholic Theology* (New York: Sheed & Ward, 1966); Max Thurian, *Mary, Mother of All Christians* (New York: Herder & Herder, 1964).
10. Martin Luther, "The Magnificat," in *The Sermon on the Mount and the Magnificat,* vol. 21 of *Luther's Works,* ed. Jaroslav Pelikan (St. Louis: Concordia Pub. House, 1956), 329.

Chapter 10

1. See, e.g., Margaret A. Krych, "Interpreting Christ to Children in Parish Education," *Word and World* 3 (1983): 62-68.
2. Alexander Schmemann, *Liturgy and Life* (New York: Orthodox Church in America, Department of Religious Education, 1974), 11; and Sophie Koulomzin, *Our Church and Our Children* (Crestwood, N.Y.: St. Vladimir's Seminary Press, 1975), 133-56.

3. Joachim Jeremias, *The Prayers of Jesus,* trans. John Bowden et al. (Philadelphia: Fortress Press, 1978), 90-92.

4. Adrian Nocent, *The Liturgical Year,* vol. 2 (Collegeville, Minn.: Liturgical Press, 1977), 60-68, 98, 108, 117-18.

5. See, e.g., William Skudlarek, *The Word in Worship* (Nashville: Abingdon Press, 1981), O. C. Edwards, Jr., *Elements of Homiletic* (New York: Pueblo Pub. Co., 1982); and Gerard S. Sloyan, *Worshipful Preaching* (Philadelphia: Fortress Press, 1984).

Conclusion

1. Translation by Ray Palmer, altered, in *Lutheran Book of Worship* (Philadelphia: Board of Pub., Lutheran Church in America, 1978), no.356.

A SECOND-THOUGHTS BIBLIOGRAPHY

Catherine of Siena. *The Prayers of Catherine of Siena*. Ed. Suzanne Noffke, O.P. New York: Paulist, 1983.

Dillard, Annie. *Teaching a Stone to Talk: Expeditions and Encounters*. New York: Harper & Row, 1982.

Duck, Ruth C. and Wilson-Kastner, Patricia. *Praising God: The Trinity in Christian Worship*. Louisville: Westminster/John Knox Press, 1999.

Haskins. Susan. *Mary Magdalen: Myth and Metaphor*. London: HarperCollins, 1993.

Henry, Avril, ed. *Biblia Pauperum: A Facsimile of the Forty-Page Blockbook*. Ithaca, New York: Cornell University Press, 1987.

Johnson, Elizabeth. *She Who Is: The Mystery of God in Feminist Theological Discourse*. New York: Crossroad, 1992.

Julian of Norwich. *A Revelation of Love*. Ed. Marion Glasscoe. Exeter Medieval English Texts and Studies. Exeter, UK: University of Exeter Press, 1993.

LaCugna, Catherine Mowry. *God for Us: The Trinity and Christian Life*. San Francisco: HarperCollins, 1991.

Lathrop, Gordon W. *Holy People: A Liturgical Ecclesiology*. Minneapolis: Fortress, 1999.

Lathrop, Gordon W. *Holy Things: A Liturgical Theology*. Minneapolis: Fortress, 1993.

Leichman, Seymour. *The Boy Who Could Sing Pictures*. New York: Doubleday & Company, 1968.

McDonnell, Colleen, and Lang, Bernhard. *Heaven: A History*. New Haven: Yale University Press, 1988.

Poole, Stafford. *Our Lady of Guadalupe: The Origins and Sources of a Mexican National Symbol, 1531-1797*. Tuscon: University of Arizona Press, 1995.

Potok, Chaim. *My Name is Asher Lev*. New York: Random House, 1972.

Ramshaw, Gail. *God beyond Gender: Feminist Christian God-Language*. Minneapolis: Fortress, 1995.

Ruether, Rosemary Radford. *Sexism and God-Talk: Toward a Feminist Theology*. 10th anniversary ed. Boston: Beacon, 1993.

Wagamese, Richard. *Keeper 'n Me*. Toronto: Doubleday Canada Limited, 1994.

LITURGICAL TEXTS

The Book of Common Prayer. New York: Seabury Press, 1979.

Book of Common Worship. Louisville: Westminster/John Knox Press, 1993.

Book of Worship. New York: United Church of Christ, 1986.

Enriching Our Worship. New York: Church Publishing Incorporated, 1998.

"The Eucharistic Liturgy of Lima." In Baptism and Eucharist: Ecumenical Convergence in Celebration. Ed. Max Thurian and Geoffrey Wainwright. Grand Rapids: Wm. B. Eerdmans, 1983.

Lutheran Book of Worship. Philadelphia: Board of Publications, Lutheran Church in America, 1978.

Lutheran Book of Worship, Ministers Desk Edition. Philadelphia: Board of Publications, Lutheran Church in America, 1978.

Praying Together. Prepared by the English Language Liturgical Consultation. Nashville: Abingdon, 1988.

Psalter for the Christian People. Ed. Gordon Lathrop and Gail Ramshaw. Collegeville: Pueblo, The Liturgical Press, 1993.

The Revised Common Lectionary. Prepared by the Consultation on Common Texts. Winfield, B.C.: Wood Lake Books, 1992.

The Rites of the Catholic Church. New York: Pueblo Publishing Company, 1976.

The Sacramentary. New York: Catholic Book Publishing, 1974.

Service Book of the Holy Eastern Orthodox Catholic and Apostolic Church. N.P.: Antiochian Orthodox Christian Archdiocese of North America, 1980.

The United Methodist Book of Worship. Nashville: The United Methodist Publishing House, 1992.

With One Voice. Minneapolis: Augsburg Fortress Publishers, 1997.

Index

I AM, 42, 53, 103
Identity, 131-32
In illo tempore, 83
Intercessory prayer, 136-37, 141-42
Invocation of the Spirit, 135

Jesus, 48-53
John, the Gospel according to, 10, 108, 151
Joshua, 49
Jung, C. G., 5, 7, 15, 54, 77, 143

King. *See* Sovereign
Kyriakon, 104
Kyrie, 105-106
Kyrios, 50, 104

Lamb, 69-72
"Lamb of God." *See* Agnus Dei
Lectionary, 151-54, 159
Lecturn, 129
Lenten gospels, 153
Light, 86-88, 92, 153
Liturgical homily, 154-57, 161
Lord, 50-51, 63, 106-107
LORD, 43, 45-46, 50, 58, 63, 106-7
"Lord, have mercy." *See* Kyrie
Lord's Day, 84-85
Lord's Prayer, 148

Mana, 114-115
Mary Magdalene, 139-40, 142-44
Mary, Virgin. *See* Virgin Mary
Melchizedek, 52, 117
Mercy, 106
Messiah, 49
Metaphor, 7-9;
   Christian, 21-23, 35; feminine, 76-78; female, 80; first person, 66-69; mingling, 9, 69-70, 88-89; second person, 69-72; third person, 72-75; verbs, 75-76
Metaphoric rhetoric, 9-10
Monarch. *See* Sovereign
Morning psalm 95, 66-69
Mother, 58-60
Mother church, 88
Mountain of God, 17, 103

Names of God:
   Father, Son, and Holy Spirit, 57; first person, 41-48; mystical, 28-31; new names,

58-60; second person, 48-53; theological, 31-32; third person, 53-56; Trinity, 56-58, 65

Nave, 104-105
New life, 134-35, 153
Nicene creed, 148-151
Nunc Dimittis, 92-93

Offering, 17-19, 23-24
Oil. *See* Unction

Paraclete, 74-75
Paschal. *See* Easter Vigil
Passover, 86,89
Person, 55, 150
Phos hilaron, 92-93
Pneuma. 54
Potter, 67
Prayer of Thanksgiving, 44, 119-120
Preaching.
   See Liturgical homily
Pronoun, *See* He; She
Psalms, 20, 27-28, 66-67, 75, 117

Rhetoric, 1-7, 11;
   Christian, 19-21
Ricoeur, Paul, 7, 168 n.4, n. 10, 170 n.10
Right hand of God, 165
Rock, 33, 67-69
Ruah, 53-54, 63

Sacred, 15-16, 25-26;
   Christian, 16-19
Sacrifice, 16, 90
Saints, 137-40, 142, 144
Sanctuary, 104
Sanctus, 107-109
Schillebeeckx, Edward, 119, 169 n. 4, 174, n. 4
Sermon, *See* Liturgical homily
She, pronoun for God, 54-55, 63
Shepherd, 67, 68
Silence, 163-165
Sin, 89, 98, 133-34, 141
Slavery, 135
Son, 50.
   See also Metaphor, second person;
   Names of God, second person
Song of Simeon.
   See Nunc Dimittis